ON THE BRIGHT cloudless morning of 6th August, 1945, after an all-clear had sounded, three American B.29 bombers flew high above the town of Hiroshima in Japan and exploded the first atomic bomb. First came the *pika*—the great blinding flash—and 70,000 people burned to death. Then followed an immense atomic blast, flattening the town to a smoking rubble, and high in the sky there rose the terrible mushroom cloud, scattering radioactive fallout all around.

Scientists had understood the true nature of the atom for less than twenty years. During the 1930s, laboratories all over Europe worked to release the energy known to exist within the atom, and in Britain and America half a million men were engaged on secret nuclear projects, driven by the fear that Hitler's Germany might get the bomb first. Led by brilliant scientists—some themselves refugees from Germany—this effort produced two small pieces of hardware, the uranium bomb nicknamed "Little Boy" and the plutonium bomb nicknamed "Fat Man". Using a fascinating range of documents from many sources, Marion Yass re-constructs not only the scientific story, but the political and espionage intrigue that lay behind Hiroshima—the first and only act of nuclear warfare. She reviews the great debate as to whether an atomic bomb should have been dropped on Hiroshima and Nagasaki at all, either from a military or moral point of view. For example, was the A-bomb tragedy so great seen against 1,850,000 Japanese deaths in World War Two? The debate about nuclear warfare, both from a strategic and moral standpoint, continues today, and it is hoped that by studying the primary sources about Hiroshima, the reader may be able to develop an informed and responsible view of his own. This is a new title in the WAYLAND DOCUMENTARY HISTORY SERIES.

Frontispiece
The first nuclear weapons: *above* "Little Boy" the type detonated over
Hiroshima (6th August, 1945) and *below* "Fat Man", detonated over
Nagasaki (8th August, 1945)

Hiroshima

Marion Yass

WAYLAND PUBLISHERS LONDON

THE WAYLAND DOCUMENTARY HISTORY SERIES

MEDIEVAL PILGRIMS *Alan Kendall*

THE REFORMATION OF THE SIXTEENTH CENTURY *L. W. Cowie*

WITCHCRAFT *Roger Hart*

PLAGUE AND FIRE *L. W. Cowie*

THE AGE OF DICKENS *Patrick Rooke*

GLADSTONE AND DISRAELI *Patrick Rooke*

ORIGINS OF WORLD WAR ONE *Roger Parkinson*

THE GREAT DEPRESSION *Marion Yass*

THE THIRD REICH *Michael Berwick*

ORIGINS OF WORLD WAR TWO *Roger Parkinson*

THE PILGRIM FATHERS *L. W. Cowie*

THE HOME FRONT *Marion Yass*

SBN 85340 159 4
Copyright © 1971 by Wayland (Publishers) Ltd
101 Grays Inn Road London WC1
Printed by The Garden City Press Limited,
Pixmore Avenue, Letchworth, Herts. SG6 1JS

Contents

The Illustrations

1 Splitting the Atom

"THERE ROSE from the bowels of the earth a light not of this world, the light of many suns in one. It was a sunrise such as the world had never seen, a great green supersun climbing in a fraction of a second to a height of more than 8,000 feet, rising ever higher until it touched the clouds, lighting up earth and sky all around with a dazzling luminosity. Up it went, a great ball of fire about a mile in diameter, changing colours as it kept shooting upward, from deep purple to orange, expanding, growing bigger, rising as it expanded . . . It was as though the earth had opened and the skies had split . . . With the flash came a delayed roll of mighty thunder, heard, just as the flash was seen, for hundreds of miles. The roar echoed and reverberated from the distant hills . . . A great cloud rose from the ground. At first it was a giant column, which soon took the shape of a supramundane mushroom (1)." *Unearthly light*

This is how an eyewitness described the first explosion of an atomic bomb. It took place in the Alamagordo desert in North America on 16th July, 1945. Even the scientists were shocked by the force, the flash and the noise of the explosion, and by the half mile crater carved out in the desert. Only six years ago had they first realized that the atom might be split, and its energy harnessed to produce nuclear power. Moreover, it was only around 1900 that the age old theory of the atom had been questioned.

For centuries, scientists had believed that every substance was made up of tiny particles grouped together in different ways. The Greeks had called these particles *atomos*, meaning "indivisible". For 2,500 years no one had imagined that the atom might be broken down into even smaller units. As a statement on Hiroshima pointed

11

Opposite: top Robert Oppenheimer and *bottom* Enrico Fermi, two scientists who helped to make the discovery of the atom bomb

out: "It was regarded as a cardinal point that the atoms of any one element could in no way be changed or converted into those of another (2)."

Discovery of radiation

Then, in 1896, a French scientist called Henri Becquerel found that the atoms of one element—uranium—were constantly giving off streams of particles, or rays. This "radiation" made nonsense of the indivisible theory of the atom. Two other famous French scientists, Marie and Pierre Curie, developed Becquerel's experiments. They found that other substances—as well as uranium—gave off radiation. They even managed to isolate radium from uranium, and so spontaneously convert the atoms of one element (uranium) into those of another (radium).

Arthur Compton, one of the scientists who helped to build the bomb, remembered how as a boy he had heard that: "Two French scientists, husband and wife, had discovered a remarkable new substance. They called it radium. This new element glowed in the dark. A yet more remarkable property . . . was that the radium kept itself warm and could do so for thousands of years. Where did the heat come from?—a continuing flow of energy! (3)"

Rutherford

Ernest Rutherford, a young New Zealander working in Montreal, Canada, was the first scientist to realize the meaning of these energy rays. In 1902 he explained that "the atoms of uranium, radium and other radioactive elements . . . were unstable and were continuously breaking up at rates which were characteristic for each element (4)."

Inside the atom

Rutherford became Professor of Physics at Manchester University in England. With the Danish physicist Niels Bohr of Copenhagen, he stopped scientists thinking of the atom as a sort of solid unbreakable billiard ball. He told how "the idea of the *nucleus* atom was developed, in which the main mass of the atom is concentrated in a positively charged nucleus of very small dimensions compared with the space occupied by the electrons which surround it (5)." Part of the nucleus had a positive electric charge, and Rutherford called this the proton. He also realized that the difference between one substance and another lay in how many protons their atoms contained. He now tried bombarding various substances with alpha particles—the rays given off by the radium atom during radiation.

In December, 1917, he wrote to Bohr from Manchester: "I have got, I think, results that will ultimately have great importance. I wish you were here to talk matters over with. I am detecting and counting the lighter atoms set in motion by alpha particles, and the results, I think, throw a good deal of light on the character and distribution of forces near the nucleus . . . I am trying to break up the atom by this method (6)."

Two years later, in 1919, an article appeared in the scientific journal *Nature*: "It appears from the latest results of Sir Ernest Rutherford on the passage of alpha particles through nitrogen, as though the nuclei of [a few] of the nitrogen atoms struck by the alpha particle were shattered by the collision. If this is so, artificial transmutation on an infinitesimal scale has already been accomplished (7)." *Changing the elements*

Rutherford had penetrated a nitrogen nucleus with particles thrown off by radium, and so turned it into the nucleus of an oxygen atom. For the first time, one element had been changed into another.

Rutherford went on with his experimental bombardment of different elements. When he became director of the famous Cavendish laboratory at Cambridge in 1921, his new students sang:

> *What's in an atom*
> *The innermost substratum?*
> *That's the problem he is working at today.*
> *He lately did discover*
> *How to shoot them down like plover*
> *And the poor little things can't get away.*
> *He uses as munitions on his hunting expeditions*
> *Alpha particles which out of Radium spring.*

Next year Niels Bohr received the Nobel prize for his work on the atom. At his award in Stockholm he said: "We not only believe the existence of atoms to be proved beyond a doubt, but we even believe that we have an intimate knowledge of the constituents of the individual atoms (8)." *Niels Bohr*

Scientists all over the world were trying to find out more about the atom. In Hamburg, Berlin and Göttingen, the German physicists Eugene Wigner, Leo Szilard, James Franck and Edward Teller were joined briefly by two brilliant young men: Robert Oppenheimer from America and Enrico Fermi from Italy. There was constant

13

interchange of information between them and the Parisian physicists. Shimizu from Japan and Pyotr Kapitka from Russia worked with Rutherford in Cambridge.

Neutrons   From the Cavendish laboratory in 1932 James Chadwick sent an article to *Nature* headed, "Possible existence of a neutron (9)." Chadwick had found the neutron—the electrically neutral part of the nucleus. This was the missing clue to the atom; it was to be vital in producing atomic fission. Bohr had found that the number of electrons or protons equalled the atomic number; similarly, Chadwick found that the number of neutrons plus the number of protons equalled the atomic mass of the element. Any elements having the same atomic number—that is, the same chemical characteristics—were said to be isotopes (chemical twins) of the same element. The picture was becoming clearer.

Energy rays   Rutherford had managed to change one element into another. But he could not free the energy locked inside the nucleus of the atom. The powerful rays thrown off during radiation had convinced scientists of the potential strength of this energy. According to Einstein's theory of relativity, the mass displaced during transmutation would be changed into energy. But, "to produce this amount of energy, other energy thousands of times greater still was necessary. The reason was that only one atom in a great many would be hit during a bombardment (10)."

Cockcroft and   The same thing happened when John Cockcroft, another of
proton   Rutherford's helpers, bombarded elements with hydrogen protons
bombardment   instead of the alpha particles of radium. Cockcroft used an "accelerator" to hurl the protons at the atoms at great speed. He managed to transmute the elements, but still found a net loss of energy. The positively charged protons were repelled on breaking into the atom by the positively charged nucleus. So the protons bounced around from one nucleus to another until they exhausted their energy.

Radioactivity   The early 1930s were years of a great leap forward in atomic science. Cockcroft broke down his atoms in 1932; in 1933 Irene Curie, Marie's daughter, and her husband Frederic Joliot found that when certain elements were bombarded with alpha rays the new atoms were radioactive. These radioactive atoms could give out more energy than the stable isotopes produced by Rutherford

14

and Cockcroft when they tried to break down the atom.

Enrico Fermi, now back in Rome discussed the Joliots' work in *Nature*. "In some cases the product atom may be radioactive ... The number of elements which can be activated, either by the impact of an alpha particle, or a proton ... is limited by the fact that only light elements can be disintegrated, owing to repulsion. This limitation is not effective in the case of neutron bombardment (11)."

Fermi and neutron bombardment

With imaginative insight, Fermi saw that the lack of charge on the neutron would let it more easily penetrate the nucleus than Rutherford's alpha rays or Cockcroft's protons.

Fermi realized that he could release the energy inside the atom if he could induce radioactivity. For this he would use Chadwick's neutrons. He sent out his helpers to find specimens of as many elements as possible. Then he worked to extract neutrons from his one precious gramme of radium. His wife watched them all "in grimy laboratory coats ... busying themselves around a complicated apparatus of vertical glass pipes several feet tall."

Fermi tries to boost radioactivity

At the end of a long process, neutrons were isolated: "Small glass tubes were used as neutron sources to irradiate all the elements ... Irradiated substances were tested for radioactivity with the Geiger counter. The radiation emitted by the neutron source would have disturbed the measurements had it reached the counter. Therefore the room where substances were irradiated, and the room with the counters, were at the two ends of a long corridor. Sometimes the radioactivity produced in an element was of short duration, and after less than a minute it could no longer be detected. Then haste was essential, and the time to cover the length of the corridor had to be reduced by swift running. Amaldi and Fermi prided themselves on being the fastest runners (12)."

In *Nature*, Fermi explained his "Radioactivity Induced by Neutron Bombardment." "Experiments have been carried out to ascertain whether neutron bombardment can produce an induced radioactivity giving rise to unstable products (13)."

The new substances formed when bombarding an element were found to be isotopes of the element lying next to the original element in the periodic table. So when Fermi came to bombard the heaviest element of all—uranium with its 92 protons—he assumed that the new element must have the atomic number 93. Certainly, chemical tests could not match this strange newcomer with any element *below* uranium in the table.

Strange new element created

A professor at the Physical Institute in Rome excitedly announced the discovery of a new heavy element. The next morning the press in New York, London and other capitals carried the news. "New Heavy Element Created," announced *The Times*: "Professor Senator Mario Orso Corbino publishes tonight in the *Giornale d'Italia* an article explaining the latest physical experiments of the Italian academician Enrico Fermi. Signor Fermi claims to have discovered a new element of atomic number 93, and therefore the most complex element known. The new element was produced when uranium of atomic number 92 was bombarded with neutrons. The new element is radioactive and is stated to be extremely unstable . . . Professor Corbino considers that the scientific possibilities opened up by this latest discovery are of incalculable importance (14)."

Water: even slower neutrons

Fermi was uncertain of this explanation. He was also furious with Corbino for his hasty publicity. He pressed on with his researches. Later the same year, 1933, he made another great step forward. His wife Laura described the exciting events of 21st October, when two of his helpers, Edoardo Amaldi and the brilliant young Bruno Pontecorvo, were testing various metals for radioactivity; they passed neutrons into special cylinders containing the metals.

Strangely, "objects around the cylinder seemed to influence its activity . . . They placed the neutron source outside the cylinder and interposed objects between them. A plate of lead made the activity increase slightly. Lead is a heavy substance. 'Let's try a light one next,' said Fermi, 'for instance, paraffin.' They took a big block of paraffin, dug a cavity in it, put the neutron source inside the cavity, irradiated the silver cylinder, and brought it to a Geiger counter to measure its activity. The counter clicked madly. The hall of the Physics building resounded with loud exclamations.

"Paraffin increased the artificially induced radioactivity of silver up to 100 times . . . Paraffin contains a great deal of hydrogen. Hydrogen nuclei are protons . . . The neutrons hit the protons in the paraffin before reaching the silver nuclei. In the collision with a proton, a neutron loses part of its energy, in the same manner as a billiard ball is slowed down when it hits a ball of its same size. Before emerging from the paraffin a neutron will have collided with many protons . . . and its velocity will be greatly reduced. This *slow* neutron will have a much better chance of being captured by a silver nucleus than a fast one—much as a slow golf ball has a better chance of making a hole than one which zooms past and may bypass it."

If Fermi was right, any other substance loaded with hydrogen would also help by slowing the neutrons down. Why not water?— after all, it was two parts of hydrogen to only one of oxygen. They hurried down to "the goldfish fountain in Corbino's private garden behind the laboratory . . . They rushed their source of neutrons and their silver cylinder to that fountain, and they placed both under water. The goldfish retained their calm and dignity, despite the neutron shower, more than did the crowd outside. The men's excitement was fed on the results of this experiment. It confirmed Fermi's theory (15)." Water, too, increased the radioactivity many times.

The "slow neutron" was a vital tool in the eventual release of atomic energy. Meanwhile, political pressure stopped many scientists from following up the great discoveries of the early 1930s. The economic depression now sweeping over Europe was a breeding ground for extremist politics. Benito Mussolini was tightening his Fascist dictatorship in Italy; the Nazi leader Adolf Hitler became Chancellor of Germany in January, 1933.

Science and politics

Free exchange of information had always been vital to the scientists. They could not work well under the new dictatorships. Fermi was shocked when Corbino claimed the discovery of element 93 as a victory for Fascism. Mussolini's men kept close watch on the scientists at the Physical Institute in Rome. When Fermi went to Stockholm in 1938 to collect his Nobel prize, he went on to the United States. He did not return to Italy.

Hitler's repressive measures, too, especially against Jewish people, forced many scientists out of Germany. Many took refuge with Niels Bohr at his Copenhagen Institute. Teller, Franck, Szilard and Wigner all left Germany for America. When Einstein packed up and went to Princeton, a French physicist remarked: "It's as important an event as would be the transfer of the Vatican from Rome to the New World. The Pope of Physics has moved, and the United States will become the centre of the natural sciences (16)."

17

Otto Hahn, a German scientist who worked on atomic research

Otto Hahn splits the uranium atom

But not all the German scientists fled from Hitler. At the Kaiser Wilhelm Institute in Berlin, Otto Hahn and his Viennese partner Lise Meitner followed Fermi's lead in bombarding elements with neutrons. Like Fermi with element 93, they were creating new elements heavier than the heaviest found in nature. In March, 1938, German troops invaded Austria. As an Austrian Jewess, Lise Meitner was now threatened by Hitler's race laws. Like Fermi, she had to escape from the country where she had done so much valuable work. She took refuge in Sweden.

In Berlin, Hahn went on with Lise's work. He noticed one substance "which, when bombarded with neutrons, did not behave like the others. This was uranium, a rare metal, and the heaviest of all the substances... All other substances except uranium divided up into a heavy substance and lightweight particles when bombarded with neutrons. But Hahn found that uranium divided up into two heavy substances (17)."

Hahn now published "positive chemical evidence to show that one, at least, of the new isotopes which were believed to be of higher atomic number than *uranium*, was in fact an isotope of the element *barium*, which has an atomic number not very different from half that of uranium (18)."

Despite Nazi restrictions, Hahn managed to send a copy of his paper to Lise Meitner in Sweden. It was she who saw the true meaning of what Hahn had found. An American journalist imagined her thoughts: "Barium! How the deuce did it get there? Where could it have come from? There definitely was not a trace of barium present when the experiment was started—and yet here it was! It was like placing a duck's egg in an incubator and suddenly seeing it hatch out into a chicken . . . Lise Meitner's thoughts wandered far afield and kept coming back to barium.

"Suddenly, what seemed at first an idle thought, to be dismissed as daydreaming, flashed into her mind—barium was *half* the atomic weight of uranium. Could it be possible that the bombardment of the uranium with the slow-speed neutron bullets split the uranium atoms in two nearly equal halves—one of which was the mysterious ghost of barium that appeared in the experiments? (19)"

Lise Meitner's inspiration

Lise Meitner's nephew, Otto Frisch, was working with Niels Bohr, also his father-in-law, at Copenhagen. He visited Sweden to see his exiled aunt. Together they worked on the figures, and decided that Lise must be right. They wrote a joint paper on 16th January, 1939, going over Hahn's experiment. Perhaps "the uranium nucleus has only small stability of form, and may, after neutron capture, divide itself into two nuclei of roughly equal size. These two nuclei will repel each other and should gain a total kinetic energy of about 200 Mev (*i.e.* 200 million electron volts from each splitting atom). The whole 'fission' process can thus be described in an essentially classical way (20)."

Before his death in 1937 Ernest Rutherford remarked that those prophesying the release of atomic energy were "talking moonshine". Two years later—only twenty years since he had first penetrated the atom and only a few months before Hitler pushed the world into war—the atom had been split.

2 The Chain Reaction Bomb

THE NEWS of the splitting of the atom early in 1939 spread swiftly. Otto Frisch rushed to Copenhagen where he just caught Niels Bohr about to leave for America. Bohr stayed with the newly arrived Fermis and attended a conference of physicists. The New York press reported: "New hope for releasing the enormous stores of energy within the atom has arisen from German experiments that are now creating a sensation among eminent physicists gathered here . . . World famous Niels Bohr of Copenhagen and Enrico Fermi of Rome, both Nobel prizewinners, are among those who acclaim this experiment as one of the most important of recent years. American scientists join them in this acclaim (21)." Fermi of course now realized that his new element 93 had been a product of splitting the uranium atom.

The release of nuclear energy was at once recognised for its potential use in an explosive weapon. As early as 1932, while James Chadwick was still discovering the neutron, a novelist had imagined an atomic explosion: "It was averred that Deposit A might produce in large quantities an element . . . that must transmute itself as radium transmutes itself, but with infinitely more violence; in fact with an explosion that would destroy all matter within a considerable range and send out waves that would exterminate all life over an indefinite area . . . Mr. Bullinger knew only that the experts had begun to whisper the words 'atomic bomb' and that . . . a single bomb could by the discharge of its electrons destroy New York (22)." Fiction could soon become fact.

But many problems remained. Power could only be built up by making the splitting of the atom cumulative. In other words, there must be a chain reaction. As Fermi told a meeting of electrical engineers, he needed "not only to have more than one neutron produced for every neutron that is absorbed in the fission, but also to be able to utilize—for producing new fissions—a large fraction of the neutrons produced. Otherwise the loss might be larger than the gain (23)."

Leo Szilard, now a refugee in the United States, worked with Fermi on the problem of how to start a chain reaction. He wrote to Joliot in Paris: "When Hahn's paper reached this country about a fortnight ago, a few of us at once got interested in the question whether neutrons are liberated in the disintegration of uranium. Obviously, if more than one neutron were liberated, a sort of chain reaction would be possible . . . This might then lead to the construction of bombs which would be extremely dangerous in general, and particularly in the hands of certain governments (24)."

Everyone knew which government he meant. Fears of Hitler's *Nazi Germany* warlike intentions had not been quelled by the Munich agreement of September, 1938. One observer at the physicists' conference in February, 1939, "went home that night very much perturbed. War at that time had become a certainty. It was equally certain to me that this was a chance the Nazis were not likely to overlook. Knowing the state of our unpreparedness, and the tremendous effort it would take to put uranium fission to work in a military weapon, it seemed almost a foregone conclusion that the Nazis would get there first. I was a frightened man (25)."

Fears grew when Hitler stopped exports of uranium ore from Nazi-occupied Czechoslovakia. The *New York Times* said: "The news has leaked out that the Nazi government had heard of the research in the American laboratories, and had ordered its greatest scientists to concentrate their energies. Every German scientist in this field, physicists, chemists and engineers, have been ordered to drop all other researches and devote themselves to this work alone at the laboratories of the Kaiser Wilhelm Institute (26)."

Enrico Fermi, with his personal knowledge of Italian dictator- *Fermi* ship, was desperate to convince Allied defence authorities of the *approaches* dangers of Nazi Germany's work on nuclear fission. He persuaded the *the U.S.A.* head of his Physics Department to contact Admiral Hooper of the U.S. Navy: "Experiments in the physics laboratories at Columbia

University reveal that conditions may be found under which the chemical element uranium may be able to liberate its large excess of atomic energy, and . . . be used as an explosive that would liberate a million times as much energy per pound as any known explosive . . . Professor Enrico Fermi who has been working on this problem will be in Washington tomorrow, and will be glad to tell you more definitely what the state of the knowledge on this subject is at present (27)."

Einstein's letter
Admiral Hooper met Fermi, but gave him polite words instead of promises. Fermi was determined to make his views known in America. In July, 1939, his colleagues Szilard and Wigner visited Albert Einstein at his Long Island home. The famous refugee signed a long letter to President Roosevelt calling for intensive research into a possible bomb: "Some recent work by E. Fermi and L. Szilard . . . leads me to expect that the element uranium may be turned into a new and important source of energy in the immediate future . . . It may become possible to set up a nuclear chain reaction in a large mass of uranium, by which vast amounts of power . . . would be generated . . . It is conceivable that extremely powerful bombs of a new type may thus be constructed (28)."

None of the scientists tried to stop the making of such a bomb. To them it was a new weapon, different in degree but not in kind from existing weapons. Their main consideration was that the enemy should not produce it first.

Isotopes: towards a chain reaction
Before Roosevelt read Einstein's letter in October, 1939, England and France had declared war on Germany. A milestone had also been passed in the scientific world. Bohr had traced the impurities in uranium which stopped a chain reaction being set up—the neutrons released in the splitting of the uranium atoms were escaping; they should have bombarded other atoms and so released still more neutrons. In a paper published the day Hitler marched into Poland, Niels Bohr and a colleague explained their work on the two known isotopes of uranium—uranium 238 and uranium 235. A few years earlier, it had been found that for every one uranium atom of atomic weight 235 found in natural uranium, there were more than a hundred atoms of atomic weight 238. "It was the U.235, Dr. Bohr and Dr. Wheeler concluded . . . that was starting the atomic fires going. The U.238 was the element that was

Left A block of Uranium 235, enough to make an atom bomb. *Right*
Uranium mined from the Belgian Congo: each sample is carefully labelled
and kept safely in a steel-made room

quenching the fires. If only a sample of the U.235 could be obtained
in pure form. But no such sample was available (29)." In other
words, Bohr found that while the U.238 atoms were gobbling up
the free neutrons, it was the U.235 which was the fissionable part of
uranium. If only the two could be separated, a chain reaction might
be got under way, using U.235 by itself.

Despite this major breakthrough, and despite the war in Europe,
President Roosevelt merely set up an Advisory Committee on
Uranium. In February, 1939, this Committee suggested a paltry
research grant. Two years passed before Roosevelt ordered
intensive research into an atomic weapon.

Meanwhile, in England in 1939, work on atomic fission had *British*
gained a slightly better start. Like Fermi, Professor G. P. Thomson *progress*
of Imperial College, London, was worried by German interest in
atomic research. Thomson also appreciated the threat to the uranium
mines in the Belgian Congo should Belgium be occupied. Whereas
Fermi had little joy from his visit to the U.S. Navy Department,

Thomson was welcomed by Henry Tizard, the head of the R.A.F. Research Department. Tizard procured an Air Ministry research grant, and one ton of uranium oxide for him to work on.

Much speculation took place in Britain about a possible uranium bomb. A *Sunday Express* journalist wrote that if a nuclear chain reaction could be produced, "the outpouring of energy would exceed anything ever known in the world. The uses to which it might be put are appalling. A nation at war might be able to wipe another nation right off the face of the earth (30)."

A science journal was almost as sensational: "Some leading physicists think that within a few months science will have produced for military use an explosive a million times more violent than dynamite. It is no secret. Laboratories in the United States, Germany, France and England have been working on it feverishly since the spring. It may not come off. The most competent opinion is divided upon whether the idea is practicable. If it is, science for the first time will at one bound have altered the scope of warfare (31)."

Scientists' doubts

In fact, leading physicists were less certain that an atomic bomb could be made. The war had coincided with progress in nuclear research, and physicists naturally wondered about a possible nuclear weapon. So far, however, all attempts to start the necessary chain reaction had failed. Professor G. P. Thomson, using his ton of uranium oxide, thought he could never start this reaction using ordinary water to boost the radioactivity as Fermi had done. After the Bohr-Wheeler paper it seemed that, if a bomb were to be made, the pure U.235 would have to be separated from the impure U.238 on an industrial scale. For even if a chain reaction could be started in natural uranium by slow neutrons, the "critical mass" of metal needed could never be loaded on an aeroplane for use as a bomb.

The doubts were voiced by Prime Minister Winston Churchill, who also wanted to kill the stories of a German super bomb: "Some weeks ago, one of the Sunday papers splashed the story of the immense amount of energy which might be released from uranium by the recently discovered chain of processes which takes place when this particular type of atom is split by neutrons . . . This might seem to portend the appearance of new explosives of devastating power . . . It is essential to realize that there is no danger that this discovery . . . will lead to results capable of being put into operation on a large

24

scale for several years . . . (32)"

In spring 1940, the outlook for the building of a British bomb was radically improved by two scientists. Rudolf Peierls had left Germany in 1929 and arrived in England in 1933. For four years he had been Professor of Mathematical Physics at Birmingham University. There he was joined by Otto Frisch who had been visiting England at the outbreak of war and decided not to return to Copenhagen. Peierls and Frisch gave up the idea of producing enough nuclear power for an atomic explosion by bombarding natural uranium with *slow* neutrons in "boilers" or "piles". But the pure uranium 235 alone, subjected to *fast* neutrons, might produce a chain reaction—and eventually a bomb. *Peierls-Frisch report*

They published their views: "The possible construction of 'super bombs' based on a nuclear chain reaction in uranium has been discussed a great deal . . . We wish here to point out and discuss a possibility which seems to have been overlooked . . . Effective methods for the separation of isotopes [of uranium] have been developed recently, of which the method of 'thermal diffusion' is simple enough to permit separation on a fairly large scale. This permits the use of nearly pure U.235 in such a bomb . . .

"We have come to the conclusion that a moderate amount of U.235 would indeed constitute an extremely efficient explosive. The behaviour of U.235 under bombardment with fast neutrons is not known experimentally, but from rather simple theoretical arguments it can be concluded that almost every collision produces fission . . . The reaction, depending on the action of fast neutrons, develops with very great rapidity (33)."

The report outlined how to separate the pure U.235 from the U.238, how to start a chain reaction, how to assemble the bomb itself, and how to work out its critical size. It even predicted the effects of atomic radiation. The bomb was still not thought to be feasible. Still, as Churchill wrote later, "the potentialities of the project were so great that His Majesty's Government thought it right that research should be carried on in spite of the many competing claims on our scientific manpower (34)." *Churchill's support*

Many atomic physicists had been diverted to work considered more vital to the war effort. Professor Thomson was developing radar at Farnborough; Mark Oliphant of Cambridge University *Maud Committee* was working on a device to protect British shipping from German mines. Both were asked to join James Chadwick and John Cockcroft on a new Uranium Sub-Committee under Henry Tizard. The Committee was soon attached to the Ministry of Aircraft Production, and became known as the Maud Committee. (Niels Bohr sent a telegram to his English friends to reassure them of his safety when the Germans occupied Denmark. The message ended: "Tell Maud Ray Kent." No one could decipher his meaning, thinking it must involve an anagram of radium. Not until Bohr came to England later in the war did the scientists learn that Maud Ray was the name of a former governess from Kent who had taught the Bohr children. Meanwhile, they named their Committee after her.)

Research problems   Their other vital tasks forced the Maud Committee members to work only part time on atomic fission. The scientists available to them in Britain were mainly aliens and refugees banned from secret projects like radar. The novelist C. P. Snow's story of early atomic work in England was not exaggerated: "All the arrangements of those first months . . . were on the pettiest scale—a handful of scientists, nearly all of them working part time, scattered round three or four university laboratories; a professor wondering whether he might spend £350 for some extra help; an improvised committee, meeting once a month, sending its minutes to the Minister in longhand. The only good scientists not yet employed were refugees and it was clear they would have to form the nucleus of Barford (35)."

The refugees working on the bomb were subject to curfew, forbidden to travel without special permission, or even to possess bicycles. Peierls and Frisch were furious at being excluded from the Maud Committee, inspired as it was by their own memorandum. Peierls had just received British citizenship; Frisch was still classified as an enemy alien, and suspected for his association with the Germans Lise Meitner and Otto Hahn.

Gaseous diffusion   Frisch and Peierls, however, went on trying to separate the two uranium isotopes, U.235 and U.238. Because these were chemically identical they had to be parted by physical means. The scientists used the fact that one was slightly heavier than the other. Their memorandum had suggested the "thermal diffusion" method. But at Birmingham the two men—joined by Klaus Fuchs who had worked in Edinburgh after leaving Germany—now concentrated on the "gaseous diffusion" method. They forced the uranium gases under pressure through membranes in hundreds of stages. Each stage yielded a slightly richer compound with more of the pure U.235 and less impure U.238.

The Maud Committee also took up Fermi's idea of starting a chain reaction in natural uranium under slow neutron bombardment. Since 1934, when Fermi had used goldfish water to boost radioactivity, it had been found that special "heavy water"—with deuterium instead of hydrogen—would do the job even better. Heavy water was made by the Norsk Hydro Company in Norway. Just before war broke out in 1939, Joliot had managed to buy the Company's entire stock of heavy water against German opposition. When France fell in June, 1940, Joliot decided to stay on in Paris. But his assistants Halban and Kowarski smuggled the twenty-six canisters of heavy water through France and across the English Channel in a small coal ship. While they were hidden first in Wormwood Scrubs Prison, then in Windsor Castle, Halban and Kowarski went to Cambridge to continue their research. *Heavy water moderator*

By the end of 1940 the Maud Committee had made great progress. Scientists at Oxford and Birmingham were sure that they could separate the two uranium isotopes—U.235 and U.238—and make a bomb.

At Cambridge Halban and Kowarski persuaded their new colleagues that a slow chain reaction was feasible in a natural uranium pile; in other words pure U.235 would not be needed. A report from the Cavendish laboratory "produced strong evidence that in a system composed of uranium oxide or uranium metal, with heavy water as the slowing down medium, a divergent slow neutron fission chain reaction would be realized if the system were of sufficient size (36)." Dr. Bretscher guessed that this slow chain reaction might also produce plutonium, the new element 94.

When the Maud Committee met in July, 1941, they took a whole month to consider the scientists' various findings, and to make a report "on the use of uranium for a bomb": "We should like to emphasize that we entered the project with more scepticism than belief, though we felt it was a matter which had to be investigated. As we proceeded we became more and more convinced that release of atomic energy on a large scale is possible, and that conditions can *Maud report: Bomb is possible*

27

be chosen which would make it a very powerful weapon of war."

They now believed they could "make an effective uranium bomb which . . . would be equivalent, as regards destructive effect, to 1,800 tons of T.N.T., and would release large quantities of radio-active substances which would make places near to where the bomb exploded dangerous to human life for a long period (37)." The report suggested that a bomb might be made by the end of 1943, and that the work on it should be given full priority.

Cherwell advises Churchill

The Maud Report said that the bomb was scientifically possible. But no attempt had yet been made to separate quantities of U.235 from U.238; no chain reaction had been started; the figures for the critical size of a bomb were still pure guesswork. Heavy investment would be needed before the theory could be proved. Decisions had to be taken on the Report. Churchill's scientific advisor, Frederick Lindemann—now Lord Cherwell—had doubts about the bomb.

But Hitler had invaded Russia in June, and German armies were sweeping everything before them. Cherwell wrote to Churchill: "People who are working on these problems consider the odds are ten to one on success within two years. I would not bet more than two to one against or even money. But I am quite clear that we must go forward. It would be unforgivable if we let the Germans develop a process ahead of us by means of which they could defeat us in war, or reverse the verdict after they had been defeated (38)."

Cherwell added that a Cabinet Minister should be appointed to look after science matters. Churchill took his advice. He wrote to General Ismay, the Secretary of the Committee of Imperial Defence: "Although personally I am quite content with the existing explosives, I feel we must not stand in the path of improvement, and I therefore think that action should be taken in the sense proposed by Lord Cherwell and that the Cabinet Minister responsible should be Sir John Anderson (39)."

Sir John Anderson: Tube Alloys

Anderson was well fitted for such a task. Now Home Secretary in the coalition War Cabinet, he had proved his administrative ability in his earlier civil service career. Moreover, in his student days he had studied physics. At Edinburgh University he had written a paper on explosives, and had even researched into the radioactivity of uranium while a postgraduate at Leipzig. He had helped to set up the Scientific Advisory Committee to the War Cabinet.

This committee now gave Anderson its reactions to the Maud Report: "We have been impressed by the unanimity and weight of scientific opinion by which the proposals are supported. The destructive power of this weapon . . . needs no emphasis . . . We are strongly of the opinion that the development of the uranium bomb should be regarded as a project of first class importance and all possible steps taken to press on with the work (40)."

Anderson took the first step. He set up a special section in the Department of Scientific and Industrial Research under W. A. Akers, the Research Director of I.C.I. The section was code-named "Tube Alloys". Akers would handle the technical side of the work while Anderson would deal with scientific administration.

The plant needed to extract the pure U.235 from natural uranium, and to build a bomb, would be enormous in size and in its demands on manpower and finance. Where was Tube Alloys to build such a plant? Cherwell wanted it to be in Britain. The Ministry of Aircraft Production was equally certain that it must be part of an American project. Not only was the expense prohibitive, but any plant in Britain would be vulnerable to German air attack.

Britain or America?

The Labour leader Clement Attlee later said: "If we had been willing to face the diverting of industrial effort . . . we had the resources and the scientific and technical skill that would have enabled us to embark on the development of the project in this country . . . We should have had to reduce our efforts in other directions, such as radar and jet propulsion. To do so at that time would not have been opportune, particularly so long as the threat of invasion lasted and while our principal centres of production were subject to air attack. Fortunately it was not necessary to make the choice. President Roosevelt had become interested in the idea of an atomic weapon . . . In October, 1941, he wrote to Mr. Churchill (41)."

Roosevelt told Churchill: "We should soon correspond or converse concerning the subject which is under study by your Maud Committee, and Dr. Bush's organization in this country, in order that any extended efforts may be co-ordinated or even jointly conducted (42)." Dr. Vannevar Bush was Director of the Office of Scientific Research and Development. Roosevelt had formed this in June to "develop broad and co-ordinated plans for the conduct of scientific research in the defence programme, in collaboration with representatives of the War and Navy Departments (43)."

Churchill took until December merely to acknowledge Roosevelt's approach. The British were reluctant to share their knowledge. Henry Tizard had led a group of British scientists to Washington the previous year. They had found the American physicists to be about six months behind them in their researches. But the Americans were working fast: they knew that the military authorities would back down unless they got results.

Work on possible methods of separating U.235 went ahead. A journalist reported: "Even now there are signs on the horizon promising considerably improved methods for the separation of U.235 in larger quantities. A number of new methods are being quietly developed in American laboratories, and one of them in particular, known as the thermal diffusion method—taking advantage of differences in temperature to separate lighter particles from their heavier components—is being thoroughly investigated as the most promising for the present (44)."

Ernest Lawrence: plutonium bomb

Tizard's mission found other close parallels with British research. Like Halban at Cambridge, Enrico Fermi was trying to start a chain reaction with natural uranium and slow neutrons. Fermi had also found that ordinary water would not slow down his neutrons sufficiently. But now he was using blocks of graphite instead of heavy water. Professor Ernest Lawrence, too, was working on natural uranium at Berkeley, California. Lawrence confirmed the suspicions of the Cambridge scientists: a new fissionable substance could be produced from the unfissionable uranium 238. He found that when the 238 atoms absorbed the neutrons, so preventing the splitting of the 235 atoms, they were themselves transformed.

In July, 1941, Lawrence reported this find: "An extremely important new possibility has been opened for the exploitation of the chain reaction with unseparated isotopes of uranium. Experiments in the Radiation Laboratory of the University of California have indicated that element 94, *i.e.* plutonium, is formed as a result of the capture of a neutron by uranium 238 . . . and furthermore that this transuranic element undergoes slow neutron fission, and therefore presumably behaves like [the pure] uranium 235.

"If this is so . . . [the impure] uranium 238 would be available for energy production, thus increasing about one hundredfold the total atomic energy obtainable from a given quantity of uranium . . . If large amounts of element 94 were available it is likely that a chain reaction with fast neutrons could be produced. In such a reaction the energy would be released at an explosive rate which might be described as a 'super bomb' (45)."

In spite of new research, most American scientists still doubted whether either the uranium bomb or the plutonium bomb could be made. But a month after making his discovery Lawrence was visited by Mark Oliphant, who was working on the isotope separation in England. Oliphant brought news of the Maud Report. Arthur Compton, working in Chicago, later told how "in early September of 1941 Ernest Lawrence called me on the phone from Berkeley. Certain new developments made him believe it would be possible to make an atomic bomb. Such a bomb, if developed in time, might determine the outcome of the war . . .

"I made a date for Lawrence to see me in Chicago . . . Lawrence began by telling briefly of new results from England and how this work had convinced him of the feasibility of making an atomic bomb using only a few kilograms of fissionable material. He described recent Berkeley experiments indicating that the bomb could be made equally well either with uranium 235, or with a new chemical element discovered in his laboratory which was soon afterwards named plutonium (46)."

Arthur Compton was as impressed as Lawrence by "the new results from England:" "Within a few years the use of bombs, or something similar, using uranium fission may determine military superiority. A fission bomb of superlatively destructive power will result from bringing quickly together a sufficient mass of element U.235. This seems to be as sure as any untried prediction based upon theory and experiment can be (47)."

Compton wrote later: "I presented the report personally to *Roosevelt acts* Vannevar Bush on 6th November, 1941 . . . Bush took the report at once to President Roosevelt (48)." Roosevelt's view of atomic research had changed since his cool reception of Einstein's letter. As his letter to Winston Churchill implied, he had already accepted its importance. He was now impressed by the effect of the British Maud Report on his own scientific advisors. He appointed an Advisory

Committee to study policy matters relating to nuclear fission. The Maud Report undoubtedly led Roosevelt to hasten work on the uranium project. The official historian has said: "Without the work of the Maud Committee, the clarity of its analysis, its synthesis of theory and practical programming, its tone or urgency, the Second World War might well have ended before an atomic bomb was dropped (49)."

Japan attacks America Roosevelt announced his decision on 6th December, 1943. Next day Japanese aircraft attacked Pearl Harbor. The *New York Times* described the great shock felt throughout America: "Sudden and unexpected attacks on Pearl Harbor by the Japanese Air Force and Navy plunged the United States and Japan into active war. The initial attack caused widespread damage and death. It was quickly followed by others . . . The news of the surprise attacks fell like a bombshell on Washington. President Roosevelt immediately ordered the country and the Army and Navy onto a full war footing (50)."

The scientists were included. War reinforced the President's decision to back the atomic research. There was one end in view—a bomb. Ten days after Japan's sudden attack it was agreed to "press as fast as possible on the fundamental physics and on the engineering planning, and particularly on the construction of pilot plants (51)."

3 The Manhattan Project

IN JANUARY, 1942, a British scientific mission braved the submarine infested Atlantic. They were sailing to America to discuss the atomic fission project with their new Allies. Akers, Peierls and Halban were astonished at the Americans' progress. Akers wrote to Anderson in London: "One thing is clear, and that is that an enormous number of people are now at work so that their resources for working out schemes quickly are vastly greater than ours (52)." After announcing his support for atomic research, President Roosevelt had lost no time in setting up the S.I. Committee to supervise the work. Industrial and university resources were enrolled.

American research progress

Progress had been made on many fronts. At Berkeley, Ernest Lawrence had devised a new kind of magnet to separate the pure uranium 235 from uranium 238. He was also working on the "thermal diffusion" process to separate the two isotopes. At Columbia the method of "gaseous diffusion" was perfected. The author of a physics textbook now wrote: "The separation of the uranium isotopes in quantity lots is now being attempted in several places. If the reader wakes some morning to read in his newspaper that half the United States was blown into the sea overnight he can rest assured that someone, somewhere, succeeded (53)."

The British were surprised to see the Americans working with such enthusiasm on unseparated uranium. They knew nothing of the plutonium discovered at Berkeley. To them the boiler method —bombarding natural uranium with slow neutrons—might create industrial power. But now the meaning of the plutonium discovery dawned on them: the boiler method could also be used to make a bomb. At the Chicago Metallurgical Laboratory, Arthur

33

Opposite: The Japanese attack on Pearl Harbor (7th December, 1941), which brought the United States into the Second World War

Compton built both graphite and heavy water piles to produce plutonium. In January he had been joined by Fermi and his colleagues from Columbia.

In May Dr. Bush's deputy, James B. Conant, announced: "All five methods will be entering very expensive pilot plant development within the next six months . . . If one discards one or two or three of the methods now, one may be betting on the slower horse unconsciously (54)."

Churchill and Roosevelt

As the official report later confirmed, "It was clear in 1942 that, even though granted very high priority, the scale upon which Tube Alloys research and development could be undertaken in the U.K. must be far smaller than in America (55)." A joint effort was now clearly to Britain's advantage. In June, 1942, Churchill visited Roosevelt at his Hyde Park home outside Washington. He strongly urged that "we should at once pool all our information, work together on equal terms, and share the results, if any, equally between us. The question then arose as to where the research plant was to be set up . . . I was very glad when the President said he thought the United States would have to do it . . . It was a hard decision to spend several hundred million pounds sterling, not so much of money as of competing forms of precious war energy, upon a project the success of which no scientist on either side of the Atlantic could guarantee (56)."

Lord Ismay—Secretary of the Committee for Imperial Defence—went with Churchill to the States. He told how "the President and the Prime Minister returned to Washington in the early morning of June 21st . . . I reported to the Prime Minister at the White House shortly after his arrival, and he told me that he had reached a very satisfactory agreement with the President about Tube Alloys (57)." But the agreement was never recorded, and did not help Churchill when Anglo-American relations grew awkward later on.

Anderson: merger needed

Anderson now wanted a clearer agreement and a definite Anglo-American merger. He advised Churchill: "The full scale plant for production according to the British method can only be erected in the United States and . . . the pilot plant also will have to be designed and erected there. The immediate effect of this would be that while certain of the more academic research work would continue to be carried on in this country, we would move our design work and the

34

personnel concerned to the United States. Henceforth, work on the bomb project would be pursued as a combined Anglo-American effort . . . We must face the fact that the pioneer work done in this country is a dwindling asset and that, unless we capitalize it quickly, we shall be rapidly outstripped. We now have a real contribution to make to a 'merger'. Soon we shall have little or none (58)."

But time was running out. On June 17th, a few days before he met Churchill outside Washington, Roosevelt had agreed to a 1943 budget of $54,000,000 to produce uranium 235 and plutonium. The Americans had reached a decisive point: research had to be backed up by large scale pilot plants. The S.I. Committee alone could not handle the problems of engineering and construction. The Army was called in. General Marshall of the Corps of Engineers was ordered to form a new "district". General Leslie R. Groves, who had supervised all United States Army construction, was now put in charge of Army activities relating to the atomic project.

Manhattan project

Groves later described how, "On August 11th, Marshall handed me the draft of a general order announcing the formation of a new district. In it he used the designation D.S.M. (Development of Substitute Materials). I objected to this term because I felt that it would arouse the curiosity of all who heard it. After some discussion we decided upon 'Manhattan' since Marshall's main office would at first be in New York City. Our choice was approved . . . and so the Manhattan Engineer District, or M.E.D., came into being (59)."

Not surprisingly, the Americans now felt less inclined toward a merger of efforts. In August, Sir John Anderson wrote to Bush with more suggestions for co-operation. In October came what James B. Conant called Bush's "masterly evasive reply" (60). The effect of the Army taking control of the atomic project was disastrous at this stage for Anglo-American relations. Scientists had lived in a world of free international exchange of views. But the Army was nothing if not nationalistic. Also, General Groves had a mania for security, and was suspicious of the number of foreigners in the British scientific teams.

Bush told Anderson nothing of the work of the M.E.D. in building the secret city where the uranium isotopes would be separated on an industrial scale. Groves recalled how he "sought

The secret city

Oak Ridge, Tennessee, the "secret city" of prefabricated homes built for those working on the separation of uranium

out a relatively undeveloped area where land was still available at a reasonable price. It had to be located well away from both coasts, so that there would be no threat of direct enemy interference . . . Travel between the site and the Washington, New York and Chicago areas had to be reasonably convenient . . . There must be an assured and considerable supply of water . . . the site should have a climate that would permit heavy construction to be carried on throughout the year (61)."

A scientist from Oak Ridge using long-handled tongs to introduce radio-active material through a concrete-walled cubicle

In September a site was found at Clinton in the Tennessee Valley. It later became known as Oak Ridge. A huge plant was built containing the miles of pipes needed for the gaseous diffusion process to extract the pure U.235. The thermal diffusion method was rejected at this point. Ernest Lawrence's giant magnet was built and housed. The wartime copper shortage meant that this had to be made from silver. The U.S. Treasury Official authorized the necessary 15,000 tons.

37

Sir John Anderson and the British scientists knew nothing of the Clinton project. Nor were they told of an even more exciting development—Fermi's first nuclear chain reaction. At Columbia, Fermi had been experimenting with his "boilers" or "piles" made of alternate graphite and uranium blocks. He hoped that the fast neutrons liberated from the fission of the U.235 atoms would escape from the uranium chunks into the graphite. There they would be slowed down. These "slow neutrons" could then bombard other U.235 atoms without being absorbed by the U.238 atoms. But the process could only work if the pile was big enough to produce enough neutrons, and if its uranium and graphite ingredients were pure.

For months the scientists worked to purify both the graphite and the uranium blocks. By mid-1942 pure graphite bricks were being made in large quantities. After he joined Arthur Compton at Chicago, Fermi began to build a new pile in a disused squash court at the University. By December 2nd the pile was ready for its final test. Fermi stood on the squash court balcony with a dozen other scientists. Arthur Compton was one of them. He described the scene as George Weil took his place by the cadmium rod that stuck out from inside the pile (cadmium absorbs neutrons; while the rod stayed in the pile, the uranium could not react):

"It was the middle of the afternoon before the preliminary tests were completed. Finally Fermi gave Weil the order to draw out the control rod another foot. This we knew meant that the chain reaction should develop on an expanding scale. The counters registering the rays from the pile began to click faster and faster until the sound became a rattle . . . Finally, after many minutes, the meters showed a reading that meant the radiation reaching the balcony was beginning to be dangerous. 'Throw in the safety rods,' came Fermi's order. They went in with a clatter. The rattle of the counters died down to an occasional click. I imagine that I can still hear the sigh of relief . . . Eugene Wigner produced a bottle of Italian wine and gave it to Fermi. A little cheer went up. Atomic power! It had been produced, kept under control, and stopped (62)."

The excitement among the scientists was understandably high. Four years after Lise Meitner had realized that the atom had been split, they had started a chain reaction: they had found a way of harnessing the energy locked inside the tiny atom. On the wall of the Chicago squash court a plaque was put up:

On 2nd December, 1942
Man achieved here
The first self-sustaining chain reaction
And thereby initiated the
Controlled release of nuclear energy.

Fermi had proved that a controllable chain reaction could be started in unseparated uranium. He had also proved that the isotope U.238 could produce a new fissionable element. For if the chain reaction could be kept going, he could make plutonium. The problem of extracting the plutonium from the uranium pile still had to be solved. Moreover, the Chicago pile had produced only enough energy to light a few bulbs.

Problems of scale

A physicist noted: "The technological gap between producing a controlled chain reaction, and using it as a large scale power source or an explosive, is comparable to the gap between the discovery of fire and the manufacture of a steam locomotive . . . As regards the plutonium separation work . . . it was necessary to draw plans for an extraction and purification plant which would separate some grammes a day of plutonium from some tons of uranium, and such planning had to be based on information obtained by microchemical studies involving only half a milligram of plutonium . . . In peacetime, no engineer or scientist in his right mind would consider making such a magnification in a single stage (63)."

Bush, Conant and General Groves felt sure that such a step was justified. A month after Fermi's successful chain reaction, they decided to build a large plutonium plant. They agreed, as Groves later wrote, that "for safety's sake, it might prove desirable to locate the production plant elsewhere than at the Tennessee site . . . no one knew what might happen, if anything, when a chain reaction was attempted in a large reactor (64)." Three large piles, each surrounded by thick walls of steel and concrete, were built several miles apart along the Columbia River at Hanford, Washington. The nearby village of Richland grew into a town of 17,000 people as it became the dormitory for the new works.

The first plutonium plant

The British began to suspect that they were being kept in the dark
by the Americans. W. A. Akers and Professor G. P. Thomson were
in Montreal, awaiting a decision on the Canadian project, which
depended on American help. Churchill's patience was running out.
He complained to Roosevelt at Casablanca early in 1943. Roosevelt
designated Harry Hopkins to deal with the problem. In February
the situation had still not improved. Sick in North Africa, Churchill
cabled to Hopkins: "Urgent decisions about our programme both
here and in Canada depend on the extent to which full collaboration
between us is restored, and I must ask you to let me have a firm
decision on United States policy in this matter very soon (65)."

Hopkins asked Dr. Bush how to deal with Churchill. He was told
that "information on this subject will be furnished to individuals—
either in this country or Great Britain—who need it, and can use it
now in the furtherance of the war effort, but that . . . information
interchanged will be restricted to this definite objective (66)." The
Americans seemed to suspect that the British were concentrating
on their piles for postwar industrial power, rather than for a bomb
to win the war.

Churchill sent Sir John Anderson to Washington to try to patch
up the quarrel. Bush was impressed with Anderson's grasp of the
scientific background. Together they made good progress, and drew
up the Quebec Agreement. After stating that the Tube Alloys project
would never be used against each other or against a third party
without the other's consent, the two sides agreed to form a Combined
Policy Committee in Washington: "There shall be complete interchange of information and ideas on all sections of the project
between members of the Policy Committee and their immediate
technical advisers. In the field of scientific research and development
there shall be full and effective interchange of information and ideas
(67)."

Winston Churchill signed the Quebec Agreement on 19th August,
1943. While seeming to create a partnership, it ended all indepen-
dent British work on the bomb. It made no mention of Britain's
earlier work on atomic research. Not all misunderstandings were
cleared up: W. A. Akers, now Chairman of Imperial Chemical
Industries, was still suspected of commercial motives. James
Chadwick was appointed scientific adviser to the British members

Los Alamos, the third "secret city" built in New Mexico where the atom
bomb was to be made

of the Policy Committee. However, the main outcome was that British scientists could join the secret American atomic research teams.

The official account later reported: "The effect of these transfers . . . was to close down entirely all work in the United Kingdom on the electromagnetic process, and to reduce almost to nothing the nuclear physical research . . . There is no doubt that this was the proper course to follow in the light of the decision . . . to give the highest priority to the production, in the shortest possible time, of an atomic bomb for use in this war. . . .

"Professor Oliphant and his team were moved to Berkeley to work with Professor Lawrence's group engaged in research on the electromagnetic isotope separation project . . . Dr. Frisch from the Liverpool nuclear physics group, and Dr. Bretscher from the corresponding Cambridge section, together with some members of their teams, were moved into the great American Tube Alloys research establishment at Los Alamos (68)."

J. Robert Oppenheimer

Los Alamos was the third secret city built for the Manhattan District. While pure U.235 was extracted at Oak Ridge and plutonium produced at Hanford, the bomb itself was made at Los Alamos. Compton at Chicago had been made responsible for developing the bomb. In June, 1942, he had appointed Dr. J. Robert Oppenheimer to lead the early phase of fast neutron research at Berkeley. Oppenheimer described how: "In later summer, I became convinced, as did others, that a major change was called for in the work on the bomb itself. We needed a central laboratory devoted wholly to this purpose where people could talk freely with each other, where theoretical ideas and experimental findings could affect each other, where the waste and frustration and error of the many compartmentalized experimental studies could be eliminated, where we could begin to come to grips with chemical, metallurgical, engineering and ordnance problems that had so far received no consideration (69)."

General Groves was convinced by the scientists. He asked Oppenheimer to direct the new phase in the development of the bomb. This decision was taken despite Oppenheimer's past links— through his former *fiancée* and his brother—with Communists. But Oppenheimer had never been a Party member himself and Groves—

usually inflexible on security—had complete faith in his reliability. Groves answered the doubts of the Manhattan security staff in a strong letter: "In accordance with my verbal directions . . . it is desired that clearance be issued for the employment of Julius Robert Oppenheimer without delay, irrespective of the information which you have concerning Mr. Oppenheimer. He is absolutely essential to the project (70)."

Together, Oppenheimer and General Groves searched for a site for the atomic bomb laboratory. The scientist took the General to a mesa (plateau) in New Mexico. In Groves' words: "We drove over the mountains toward Santa Fe . . . As we approached Los Alamos, we came upon a boys' boarding school that occupied part of the area. It was quite evident that this would be an isolated site, with plenty of room for expansion (71)." *Los Alamos: the third secret city*

Ironically, the best account of the secret city's birth comes from Oppenheimer's own evidence, ten years later, when he faced a baseless charge of treason: "The last months of 1942 and 1943 had hardly enough hours to get Los Alamos established . . . To recruit staff I travelled all over the country talking with people who had been working on one or another aspect of the atomic energy enterprise . . . The notion of disappearing into the New Mexico desert for an indeterminate period and under quasi military auspices disturbed a good many scientists.

"But there was another side to it. Almost everyone realized that this was a great undertaking. Almost everyone knew that if it were completed successfully and rapidly enough, it might determine the outcome of the war. Almost everyone knew that this job, if it were achieved, would be a part of history (72)."

In March, 1943, the first scientists arrived in Los Alamos. After the Quebec Agreement they were joined by the British team. The British scientists now learned for the first time of American progress in the gaseous diffusion method of separating isotopes, and in making plutonium. James Chadwick, the intellectual academic, managed to get on surprisingly well with the tough, bluff, General Groves. Oppenheimer himself was responsible not only for the speed of technical progress, but for the high morale of the secret city. Fermi's wife described how "Oppie, as his friends called him, went around the Technical Area with his pipe in his mouth, and in his quiet way asked questions without seeming to ask, was kept informed about all the work, and was in close touch with everyone. His enthusiasm and zeal spurred others to do their best, and most of the success of the project is due to him (73)."

Niels Bohr

The other best known figure on the campus was "Nicholas Baker", alias Niels Bohr. Bohr had remained in Copenhagen after the German occupation of Denmark. He was determined to make his Institute a haven for refugee German scientists. He had destroyed or hidden evidence of his atomic researches. Early in 1943 James Chadwick managed to get a message to him. Written on microfilm, it was concealed in the handle of a doorkey: "I have heard in a roundabout way that you have considered coming to this country if the opportunity should offer . . . There is no scientist in the world who would be more acceptable both to our university people and to our general public . . . I have in mind a particular problem in which your assistance would be of the greatest help (74)."

Bohr knew nothing of the Frisch-Peierls note on the chain reaction bomb, or of Fermi's successful chain reaction experiment. He still felt that the material for a bomb could not be produced. But he knew what Chadwick's letter meant. He replied, using the same key to hide his letter, that he felt duty bound to remain in Copenhagen. "But neither such duties, nor even the dangers of retaliation against my colleagues and family, would have sufficient weight to hold me here if I felt that I could be of real help in any other way. I feel convinced that any immediate use of the latest marvellous discoveries of atomic physics is impractical. However, there may, and perhaps in the near future, come a moment when things look different and when I might be able modestly to assist in the restoration of international collaboration in human progress. At that moment I shall gladly make an effort to join my friends (75)."

Bohr flees Denmark

The moment came that August, 1943, when Hitler imposed martial law on occupied Denmark. With the tide of the war turning against them in North Africa and Russia, Germany's demands on her occupied territories were increasing. Hitler was determined to crush the Danish resistance movement in which Bohr was involved. Bohr realized that he was in danger of being deported to Germany. With his wife he escaped at the last minute in a fishing boat to Sweden. His four sons followed the next day, and a baby grandchild was smuggled out in the shopping bag of a Swedish embassy official. James Chadwick had arranged with the British Secret Service to transport Bohr to England. The large 58-year-old Danish scientist flew over in the bomb bay of a Mosquito aeroplane. He arrived in England unconscious. His forehead was so high that his earphones did not reach his ears. He had not heard the pilot tell him to use his oxygen equipment.

In England, Bohr told the scientists the meaning of the Maud Ray telegram. Astounded to learn of the developments in atomic research, he agreed to go in December with his physicist son to the United States. He was to assist the British Director of Tube Alloys. He spent some time in Washington but worked mainly in the secret city of Los Alamos. Laura Fermi described him as "a heavy set man with a big, grey-haired head and stooping shoulders who always looked preoccupied. When he walked about town he did not seem to see where he was going, and when he talked only a whisper came from his mouth (76)."

Bohr's pseudonym—Nicholas Baker—was one of many security *Security* precautions imposed on the whole Manhattan project. All scientists were sworn to utter secrecy. At a party given on 3rd December, 1942, Laura Fermi could not understand the congratulations showered on her husband. Not until the end of the war did she learn that this was the morrow of Fermi's first chain reaction. Security was even stricter in the three secret towns. As General Groves said, "Life in each had its own unique aspects but certain factors were common to them all—isolation, security restrictions, spartan living conditions, monotony (77)."

Scientists, engineers, and all workers and their families, were forbidden to tell their families in the outside world where they were. All incoming mail was taken through box numbers; all outgoing letters were censored. The new cities were fenced in. Passes had to be shown on entry and exit. The scientists were accompanied by bodyguards and subject to curfew. Laura Fermi described how Groves "designated some half dozen of his most valuable charges to be protected by a member of the Army Intelligence in plain clothes...The rules General Groves had set could have been chosen by a wise mother for her teenage daughter. Enrico was not to walk by himself in the evening, nor was he to drive without escort (78)."

45

Suspicions were aroused in the outside world. The U.S. Treasury had been surprised at Ernest Lawrence's request for 15,000 tons of silver. The Office of Defence Transportation was taken aback by Hanford's request for 500 buses required to carry workers to the factories and piles spread over ninety square miles. And the publishers of a book on nuclear physics were bewildered to receive more than 1,000 orders from the tiny village of Richland.

The Senate investigates

Politicians, too, were worried by the blank cheque given by Congress to the Manhattan District. Billions of dollars, thousands of tons of concrete, steel and copper were being poured into the project. No end product was visible. Harry S. Truman persuaded Congress to set up a special Senate Committee to investigate matters. He became its chairman. He "sent investigators into Tennessee and the State of Washington with instructions to find out what certain enormous constructions were and what their purpose was. At that time, Secretary Stimson had phoned me to say that he wanted to have a private talk with me . . . As soon as he arrived, I learned that the subject he had in mind was connected with the immense installations I had sent the Committee representatives to investigate. 'Senator,' the Secretary told me, 'I can't tell you what it is, but it is the greatest project in the history of the world. It is most top secret. Many of the people who are actually engaged in the work have no idea what it is, and we who do would appreciate your not going into those plants.' (79)"

Truman called off the investigations. He did not learn what the plants were for until he became President on Roosevelt's death. The secret was extraordinarily well kept. After the war one politician commented, "The long, expensive and tedious work, involving the finest scientific brains the nation could command and tens of thousands of workers, had been the best kept secret of the entire war (80)."

4 Making the Hardware

THE INTRICATE security precautions of the Manhattan project were *Fear of* meant to keep all knowledge of Allied work on the bomb from the *Germany* Germans. The Los Alamos scientists were working against time: Hitler must not make the weapon first. As J. Robert Oppenheimer wrote: "We had information in those days of German activity in the field of nuclear fission. We were aware of what it might mean if they beat us to the draw . . . The consensus of all our opinions, and every directive that I had, stressed the extreme urgency of our work, as well as the need for guarding all knowledge of it from our enemies (81)."

The fear that had driven Leo Szilard to Einstein, and G. P. Thomson to Henry Tizard in 1939, still remained. Germany's invasion of Norway gave Hitler access to the Norsk Hydro heavy water plant. British intelligence reported to the Ministry of Economic Warfare that the Germans ordered a 3,000 lb. annual production increase in 1940, and a further increase to 10,000 lb. in 1942. Combined with the banning of the export of ore from the Czech uranium mines, this must mean that the Germans were building atomic piles.

Joseph Goebbels' diaries, discovered after the war, showed how right the Allies were to fear German progress. An entry of March, 1942, reads: "I received a report about the latest developments in German science. Research in the realm of atomic destruction has now proceeded to a point where its results may possibly be used in the present war . . . German science is at its peak in this matter. It is essential that we should keep ahead of everybody, for whoever introduces a really revolutionary novelty in this war has the greatest chance of winning it (82)."

The British were determined to sabotage the German effort. Two abortive attempts were made to parachute men down onto the mountainous ground near the Norsk Hydro plant. At last in February, 1943, á Norwegian team was safely dropped. Their leader told how they crossed the mountains on skis, crossed a frozen river as the ice was breaking, and "clambered up sheer rock face for about 150 metres . . . We advanced within 500 metres of the factory's gate . . . Here we waited and watched the relief guard coming up from the bridge. Cautiously we advanced to some store sheds . . . During our search for the cable tunnel, which was our only method of entry we became separated from one another. Finally I found the opening and, followed by only one of my men, crept in over a maze of tangled pipes. Through an opening under the tunnel's ceiling we could see our target.

"Every minute was now valuable. We two decided to carry out the demolition alone. We found the door into the high-concentration plant open, went in and took the guard completely by surprise. I began to place the charges. The models on which we had practised in England were exact duplicates of the real plant. I coupled the fuses. There was still no sign of alarm from the yard. We lit both fuses. I ordered the captive guard to run for safety (83)."

When the story could be made public, the *Times* told how "the nine Norwegians, trained in England for sabotage work, were dropped by parachute from a Stirling bomber, forced an entry to the plant, and demolished the most important parts of the heavy water apparatus with explosives. The Germans were not able to restart production before their capitulation (84)."

But the fear of a German bomb was not destroyed with the heavy water plant. When Niels Bohr escaped to England later that year, he thought that the Germans were still considering the use of atomic energy. Despite Allied landings in Italy and talk of a "second front", the suspicion remained that Hitler had a super weapon up his sleeve. General Sir Alan Brooke told a friend that he "had some nasty moments wondering whether the Boche would forestall us with the atomic bomb and snatch victory from under our noses (85)."

British agents had been spying on the German scientists. The Manhattan District now joined the fray. General Groves set up a special unit called Alsos—the Greek word for groves—under

Lieutenant-Colonel Boris Pash. Alsos was ordered to report on "scientific developments in progress in enemy research and development establishments, which are directed towards new weapons of war or new tactics . . . and to secure all important persons, laboratories and scientific information immediately upon their becoming available to our forces before their dispersal or destruction (86)."

Pash led teams into Italy, France and Germany, following the Allied armies as they overran enemy territory. They reached Germany's research units at Strasbourg in November, 1944. Groves learned from them "that Hitler had been apprised in 1942 of the possibilities of a nuclear weapon. Nevertheless, all evidence from Strasbourg clearly pointed to the fact that . . . the enemy's efforts to develop a bomb were still in the experimental stages, and greatly increased our belief that there was little probability of any sudden nuclear surprise from Germany (87)."

The fear of an enemy bomb had after all been exaggerated. Meanwhile, the prospect of an Allied bomb increased. Vast though they were, the problems of separating the uranium isotopes and producing plutonium had been overcome. Laboratory research to perfect these techniques went on; work in the factories and piles of Oak Ridge and Hanford turned theory into industrial practice. *"Critical Mass"*

The next stage was actually to build a bomb. First of all, its optimum size had to be decided. If it was too small, too many neutrons would escape; if it was too large an explosion would occur too early. The physicist historian of the project explained: "It is impossible to prevent a chain reaction from occurring when the size exceeds the critical size. For there are always enough neutrons to initiate the chain. Thus until detonation is desired, the bomb must consist of a number of separate pieces, each one of which is below the critical size . . . To produce detonation, the parts of the bomb must be brought together rapidly (88)."

The scientists had first to find the exact critical mass necessary for a bomb. Second, they had to find a swift method of detonation. While Otto Frisch worked on the fissile material, "tickling the dragon" to find the exact amount needed to produce the desired explosion, Groves looked for an explosive expert: "The man we needed should have a sound understanding of both practical and theoretical ordnance—high explosives, guns and fusing—a wide *"Tickling the Dragon"* acquaintance and an excellent reputation among military ordnance people; a reasonably broad background in scientific development; and an ability to attract and hold the respect of scientists (89)." Commander William S. Parsons, a naval officer with ordnance and technical experience, joined the Los Alamos team.

Parsons and Niels Bohr worked together on the bomb. As the Atomic Energy Commission later explained, "The exigencies of production, the innumerable small problems which confronted the physicists, had led them away from some of the fundamental problems of the bomb. Bohr's interest gave rise to new . . . activities which cleared up many unanswered questions. He instigated some of the most important experiments . . . His criticism enlivened discussions on bomb assembly, and he participated very actively in the design of the initiator (90)."

Trigger method   In the case of the uranium bomb, the best initiator (method of detonation) was agreed: "The most straightforward proposal for the bomb's design utilized the gun assembly method to bring a critical mass of fissionable material together. In this method, one subcritical mass of fissionable material was fired as a projectile into a second subcritical mass of fissionable material, the target producing momentarily a supercritical mass which would explode (91)."

Implosion   But the physicists quickly saw that this simple gun method could
method   not be used for the plutonium bomb. Plutonium reacts much more easily than uranium; the reaction might begin too quickly and fizzle out before the bomb had reached its most reactive state. The subcritical masses would have to be brought together even faster than the gun method could achieve. Bohr worked with Dr. S. H. Neddermeyer on this problem. Their solution, as Groves explained, "utilized the effects of implosion, by directing the blast of conventional high explosives inward toward a quantity of fissionable material. The force of this blast literally squeezed the material together until it reached a critical mass and detonated (92)."

By the autumn of 1944 the atomic bomb was still only on the drawing board. The war in Europe, at least, would clearly be over before it could be produced. When President Roosevelt and Churchill met again near Washington in September, it was the Japanese against whom they considered using it. There was still doubt about its production. Admiral Leahy attended a meeting the same month when the use of an atomic weapon was discussed: "While Professor Bush had evidently convinced the President and the Prime Minister of the effectiveness of his project and had been given great sums of money for its development, his presentation was not completely convincing to me . . . I still did not have much confidence in the practicability of the project (93)."

But in December, 1944, Groves reported to General Marshall: "The first bomb . . . should be ready about 1st August, 1945 . . . We should have sufficient material for the first implosion type bomb sometime in the latter part of July. The plan of operation, while based on the more certain gun type bomb, also provides for the use of the implosion type bombs when they become fully available (94)." In February, 1945, two trucks carrying twenty cans of plutonium nitrate were driven from the factory at Hanford to Los Alamos. Work on assembling the plutonium bomb could now go ahead.

General Groves' memo implied that ways of using the bomb were already being considered. He also told Marshall that "the 509th composite group, 20th Air Force, has been organized and it is now undergoing training as well as assisting in essential tests (95)." In the spring of 1944 Groves had called on General Henry ("Hap") Arnold of the Army Air Force. He "discussed the whole situation with him, including our prospects for success and the date upon which the bomb would probably be ready . . . In calling upon him at this time I was, of course, assuming that our work would be successful . . . We began to prepare for combat operations a year before we knew that we could produce an atomic explosion (96)."

General Arnold chose his chief pilot, Colonel Paul W. Tibbets, *Air crew* from a list submitted to him by Colonel Roscoe Wilson, Manhattan's *training* air project officer. Colonel Tibbets had flown Eisenhower on missions. He was an experienced bomber pilot over Europe, with a fine reputation for leadership. In September Tibbets handpicked the men for the specially formed 509th group, and started a strict training schedule for them at their camp in Wendover Field, Utah, near Salt Lake City. They flew B.29 bombers with enlarged bomb bays, stripped of armaments to lighten them for a swift getaway from the explosion.

Group Captain Leonard Cheshire, a British airman who visited

Wendover Field, noted how the crews were "isolated from the world, undergoing an intensive course of training. The problems they had to undergo were twofold: first to drop the bomb accurately, and second to avoid the effects of the explosion . . . As soon as it was clear, the aeroplane was to turn as rapidly as possible on to a reciprocal course and fly off at a speed of seven miles a minute. This manoeuvre was practised by the crews for weeks on end, and there was no doubt that they could follow the routine as well as they could the path to the cookhouse door . . . So long as the weather was clear they could guarantee delivering the bomb within 200 yards of the aiming point (97)."

Security at the training camp was almost as stringent as at Los Alamos, where the bomb was being built. If the pilots asked why they were dropping single 1,000-lb. bombs known as "pumpkins" instead of the usual clusters dropped in bombing raids, they were told they were practising dropping land mines on Formosa. The pear shape of the plutonium bomb led it to be called "Fat Man". The more compact uranium bomb was known as "Little Boy" or "Thin Man".

Tinian island base

Thus, by the end of 1944, the physicists could give a date for the production of an atomic bomb. The aircrews' training scheme at Wendover was completed. General Groves began to plan for an operating base in the Pacific. He asked Commander Ashworth to find the best spot in the Mariana Islands for an attack on Japan. The

52

Above: A United States B.29 bomber on a test flight (carrying a small rocket-propelled plane). This type was used to drop the atom bomb

islands of Okinawa and Iwo Jima were still areas of fierce fighting between American and Japanese troops. Tinian lay slightly further from the mainland, but had been conquered. Its Japanese aerodrome and roads made it suitable for the operations of the 509th. Builders and engineers began to set up camp there. The first contingent of the 509th arrived in the middle of May, 1945. They were followed by engineers and scientists from Los Alamos.

A journalist who joined them wrote, "New Yorkers like myself found themselves at home on Tinian. Its roads were laid out along the lines of Manhattan Island. The small atom town of twenty-one raised tents, where I lived with the atomic bomb scientists during my stay at Tinian, was located somewhere in the vicinity of 'Times Square'. The flying field from which the B.29s took off was located somewhere in 'Upper Manhattan'. 'Broadway' and 'Eighth Avenue' were the two main thoroughfares, along which at all hours of the day and night the atomic bombers rumbled in jeeps and trucks to and from the bomb assembly area (98)."

Group Captain Cheshire reported that "The 509th was more or less secluded from the rest of the island. It had its own administrative and living quarters, its own compound and dispersal area (99)." The crews continued their intensive training with the B.29s, often flying alone over Japan to accustom the Japanese to the sight of solitary planes. One of the Los Alamos physicists watched them: "You could see ten or twelve planes at a time, spaced a couple of miles apart. As fast as the near plane would land, another would appear on the edge of the sky (100)."

At home, enough uranium had been separated—using both the gaseous diffusion and the electromagnetic plants—to make a single bomb. Enough plutonium had at last been extracted from the Hanford piles to make another two bombs. Secretary of State Henry L. Stimson recalled: "In the spring of 1945 it became evident that the climax of our prolonged atomic effort was at hand. By the nature of atomic chain reactions it was impossible to state with certainty that we had succeeded until a bomb had actually exploded in a full-scale experiment . . . This was to be done at the Almagordo Reservation in New Mexico . . . What had begun as a well founded hope was now developing into a reality (101)." The scientists were sure that the uranium bomb would explode; but the implosion

The "Trinity" test bomb

53

method needed on the plutonium bomb was less certain. The test was therefore planned for "Fat Man", the plutonium bomb.

In his notes for his history of the project, Henry Smyth wrote: "The end of June finds us expecting from day to day to hear of the explosion of the first atomic bomb devised by man (102)." Laura Fermi reported that "early in July men had started to disappear from the mesa and the word 'Trinity' floated with insistence in the air . . . By July 15th nobody who was anybody was left in Los Alamos (103)."

A journalist's
account

Laura Fermi did not know why so many people were leaving Los Alamos for Albuquerque. One of the few non-scientists who did know was a reporter from the *New York Times* who had been engaged by Groves to cover the project. He also knew that "Trinity" was the code name given to the test. The reporter was permitted to watch this on the appointed day: "I joined a caravan of three buses, three automobiles and a truck carrying radio equipment at 11 p.m. on Sunday, July 15th at Albuquerque. There were about ninety of us in that strange caravan, travelling silently and in the utmost secrecy through the night . . . With the exception of myself it consisted of scientists from the highly secret atomic bomb research and development centre . . . The caravan wound its way slowly over the tortuous roads, overlooking the precipitous canyons of Northern New Mexico . . .

"The end of our trail was reached after we had covered about five miles on the dirt road . . . We were in the middle of the New Mexico desert. The bomb test site, Zero, was a little to the left. We gathered in a circle to listen to directions on what we were to do at the time of the test, directions read aloud by the light of a flashlight: 'All personnel whose duties did not specifically require otherwise to lie prone on the ground with the head away from Zero. Do not watch for the flash directly but turn over after it has occurred . . . The hazard from ultraviolet light injuries to the skin is best overcome by wearing long trousers and shirts with long sleeves.'

"The assistant to the scientific director handed each of us a flat piece of coloured glass such as is used by arc welders to shield their eyes . . . Someone produced sunburn lotion and passed it around. It was an eerie sight to see a number of our highest ranking scientists seriously rubbing sunburn lotion on their faces and hands in the

54

Opposite: The dawn of the atomic age: the first explosion of the atom bomb in New Mexico (16th July, 1945)

pitch blackness of the night, twenty miles away from the expected flash . . . The bomb was set on a structural steel tower 100 feet high . . . S.10 was the control centre. Here Professor Oppenheimer, as scientific commander-in-chief, issued orders (104)."

General Farrell, also at control, described how "Dr. Oppenheimer grew tenser as the last seconds ticked off. He scarcely breathed. He held on to a post to steady himself. For the last few seconds, he stared directly ahead and then when the announcer shouted— 'Now!'—and there came this tremendous burst of light, followed shortly thereafter by the deep growling roar of the explosion, his face relaxed into an expression of tremendous relief.

Brighter than the sun

"The lighting effects beggared description. The whole country was lighted by a searing light with the intensity many times that of the midday sun. It was golden, purple, violet, grey and blue. It lighted every peak, crevasse and ridge of the nearby mountain range . . . Thirty seconds after the explosion came first the air blast pressing hard against the people, to be followed almost immediately by the strong sustained, awesome roar which warned of doomsday. The tension in the room let up and all started congratulating each other. Everyone sensed, 'This is it!' No matter what might happen now, all knew that the impossible scientific job had been done. Atomic fission would no longer be hidden in the cloisters of the theoretical physicists' dreams (105)."

General Groves sent Secretary of War Stimson a report of the test: "At 0530, 16th July, 1945, in a remote section of the Alamagordo Air Base, New Mexico, the first full scale test was made of the implosion type atomic fission bomb. For the first time in history there was a nuclear explosion. The bomb was not dropped from an airplane, but was exploded on a platform on top of a 100 foot high steel tower. The test was successful beyond the most optimistic

General Groves reports

expectations of anyone. I estimate the energy generated to be in excess of the equivalent of 15,000 to 20,000 tons of T.N.T. . . . . a huge ball of fire was formed which lasted for several seconds. This ball mushroomed and rose to a height of over 10,000 feet before it dimmed. The light from the explosion was seen clearly at Albuquerque, Santa Fe, and other points about 180 miles away. The sound was heard to the same distance in a few instances but generally to about 100 miles . . . A crater from which all vegetation had vanished, with a diameter of 1,200 feet was formed . . . The steel from the tower was evaporated (106)."

The success of the "Trinity" test surprised even the scientists. At a poll taken before the explosion, many had guessed that the yield of the bomb in terms of tons of T.N.T. would be a few thousands. Some had put it as low as several hundreds.

"Little Boy"   "Fat Man" had been successfully tested. The scientists were certain that "Little Boy" would explode. In any case, uranium 235 was so precious and took so long to produce that it could not be spared for a test. Some of the parts of the uranium bomb were stowed on board the cruiser *Indianapolis* on the morning of the test. They arrived at the island of Tinian on July 26th. The *Indianapolis* was sunk by a Japanese submarine on her return voyage. The vital component of the bomb was taken by air. Group Captain Cheshire described how, "One day towards the end of July, a Green Hornet landed at Honolulu on the way to Tinian carrying nothing but two officers and a peculiar yellow box. It was a very peculiar box. What it had inside it was the vital part of the atom bomb (107)."

On arrival at Tinian the box became the responsibility of Commander Parsons, who had flown from Los Alamos to supervise the final assembly of the bomb. The parts were taken to the compound in the area belonging to the 509th: "It was in this compound, with the three barbed wire guarded enclosures, that the work of assembling and testing the bomb was carried out. In the third enclosure was the inner sanctum, a nissen hut, air conditioned against the damp and humidity. There, amongst a disorderly mess of equipment and test gear, lay the atom cores before their final assembly into bombs (108)."

The pilots were on standby and the bomb in place. If and when the order should come, all would be ready.

5 The Decision to Bomb Japan

COLONEL PASH and his Alsos secret agents did much to reassure the Manhattan District. There seemed little doubt that Hitler had fallen behind in the race to build an atomic weapon. But a new fear overtook the scientists. Leo Szilard remembered: "During 1943 and part of 1944 our greatest worry was the possibility that Germany would perfect an atomic bomb before the invasion of Europe . . . In 1945 when we ceased worrying about what the Germans might do to us, we began to worry about what the government of the United States might do to other countries (109)."

The first scientist to be worried was the Dane, Niels Bohr. He saw that the atomic bomb would create new world problems. As the war progressed, suspicion of Joseph Stalin's Russian dictatorship grew. Bohr knew that tension between Russia and her Western Allies would probably develop after the war—the more so if Russia was left to find out about the bomb for herself. The secret must be shared. Bohr talked to Roosevelt's advisors and wrote to Sir John Anderson in London. Anderson, much impressed, contacted Winston Churchill in March, 1944, echoing his friend's sentiments: "No plans for world organization which ignore the potentialities of Tube Alloys can be worth the paper on which they are written. Indeed, it may well be that our thinking on these matters must now be on an entirely new plane (110)."

Bohr pleads for caution

Churchill merely scribbled—"I do not agree"—on Anderson's note. He granted Bohr an interview when he arrived in England the following month. But he was distracted by plans for the D-Day landings. He was unimpressed by the scientist's low voiced circumlocutions. On returning to the United States, Bohr in desperation wrote a long memorandum to President Roosevelt: "A weapon of unparalleled power is being created . . . Quite apart from the question of how soon the weapon will be ready for use and what role it may play in the present war, this situation raises a number of problems which call for most urgent attention. Unless, indeed, some agreement about the control of the use of the new active materials can be obtained, any temporary advantage, however great, may be outweighed by a perpetual menace to human security (111)."

Churchill meets Roosevelt Roosevelt and Churchill met at Hyde Park, Washington, in September, 1944. Neither was moved by Bohr's plea for caution. The two leaders had the first formal, if tentative, talks on what to do with the bomb: "The suggestion that the world should be informed regarding Tube Alloys, with a view to an international agreement regarding its control and use, is not accepted. The matter should continue to be regarded as of the utmost secrecy; but when a 'bomb' is finally available, it might perhaps, after mature consideration, be used against the Japanese." Also, "enquiries should be made regarding the activities of Professor Bohr, and steps taken to ensure that he is responsible for no leakage of information—particularly to the Russians (112)."

Fuchs and Pontecorvo These Hyde Park talks were not made public. Bohr was, as usual, discreet about his political campaigning. Nevertheless most of the physicists agreed that the politicians were unwise to keep the atomic weapon secret from their Allies. One of them dramatically took things into his own hands. In February, Klaus Fuchs, working with Peierls at Los Alamos, passed on information about the new weapon to a Russian spy, Harry Gold. Whatever his motives, Fuchs—like Bruno Pontecorvo at the Canadian atomic plant who also turned spy— had access to atomic secrets valuable to the Russians.

Other physicists worried about the bomb took a less extreme course. A group at the Metallurgical Laboratory in Chicago, including Leo Szilard and James Franck, had also grown disturbed about the future of the bomb. The first meeting of the United Nations Assembly was planned for April, 1945, in San Francisco. How could the powers decide the future of the world if not all of them knew about the bomb? Leo Szilard once again approached the great Einstein. He asked him to sign a petition to the President cautioning him about the use of the bomb. While the petition lay on his desk in April, Roosevelt died.

Harry S. Truman, the new President, knew no more about the bomb than he had done when asked to call off his investigations at Oak Ridge and Hanford. He now received a note from Stimson: "I think it is very important that I should have a talk with you as soon as possible on a highly secret matter. It has such a bearing on our present foreign relations . . . that I think you ought to know about it without much further delay (113)."

In his memoirs, Truman wrote under the dateline April 25th: "At noon I saw Secretary of War Stimson in connection with the urgent letter he had written . . . I listened with absorbed interest, for Stimson was a man of great wisdom and foresight. He went into considerable detail in describing the nature and the power of the projected weapon. If expectations were to be realized, he told me, the atomic bomb would be certain to have a decisive influence . . . And if it worked, the bomb in all probability would shorten the war . . . The Secretary appeared confident of the outcome and told me that in all probability success would be attained within the next few months. He also suggested that I designate a committee to study and advise me of the implications of this new force (114)." *Truman's Interim Committee*

Truman took Stimson's advice. He set up the Interim Committee. This included Stimson and his deputy George Harrison, James Byrnes the President's new Secretary of State, Ralph Bard the Under-Secretary of the Navy, Karl Compton President of the Massachussetts Institute of Technology, and Dr. Vannevar Bush. An advisoɩy panel of four scientists was attached to the new Committee: Robert Oppenheimer, Enrico Fermi, Ernest Lawrence and Arthur Compton. The scientists were brought nearer the political arena.

The European war was over before the Interim Committee met. Germany surrendered unconditionally in 1945. Hitler committed suicide in Berlin. Truman announced the Allied victory on May 9th, and then "called on Japan to surrender unconditionally, and urged the Japanese to do so by stating that, otherwise, utter destruction awaited them . . . Mr. Truman warned the American people . . . to 'work, work, work . . . the West is free but the East is still in bondage to the treacherous tyranny of the Japanese. When the last Japanese division has surrendered unconditionally, then only will our fighting job be done' (115)." The Burmese and Far Eastern campaigns had been the toughest of the war. The bitter, barbarous fights at Batuan and Corregidor in 1942 were as fresh in American minds as the attack on Pearl Harbor. Such memories gave force to the agreement of Churchill and Roosevelt at Casablanca that the Allied war aim should be the unconditional surrender of each enemy.

Secretary of War Stimson urged the new Interim Committee "to recommend action that may turn the course of civilization. In our hands we expect soon to have a weapon of wholly unprecedented destructive power. Today's prime fact is war. Our great task is to bring this war to a prompt and successful conclusion. We may assume that our new weapon puts in our hands overwhelming power. It is our obligation to use this power with the best wisdom we can command (116)."

Decision to bomb Japan

Arthur Compton recalled: "Throughout the morning's discussions it seemed a foregone conclusion that the bomb would be used ... At the luncheon following the morning meeting I was seated at Mr. Stimson's left. In the course of the conversation I asked whether it might not be possible to arrange a non-military demonstration of the bomb in such a manner that the Japanese would be so impressed that they would see the uselessness of continuing the war. The Secretary opened this question for general discussion by those at the table.

"Various possibilities were brought forward. One after the other it seemed necessary that they should be discarded. If a bomb were exploded in Japan with previous notice, the Japanese air power was still adequate to give serious interference . . . If during the final adjustments of the bomb the Japanese defenders should attack, a faulty move might easily result in some kind of failure. Such an end to an advertised demonstration of power would be much worse than if the attempt had not been made.

"It was now evident that when the time came for bombs to be used we should have only one of them available, followed afterwards by others at long intervals. We could not afford the chance that one of them might be a dud. If the test were made on some neutral territory, it was hard to believe that Japan's determined and fanatical military men would be impressed. If such an open test were made first, and failed to bring surrender, the chance would be gone to give the shock of surprise. Though the possibility of a demonstration that would not destroy human life was attractive, no one could suggest a way in which it could be made so convincing that it would be likely to stop the war (117)."

James Byrnes also explained: "We feared that, if the Japanese were told that the bomb would be used on a given locality, they might bring our boys who were prisoners of war to that area (118)."

So the Interim Committee wanted the atomic bomb to hit Japan without warning. Further, it should be dropped on a combined military and residential target to produce the maximum psychological shock. The decision was unanimous, though Bard later changed his mind and thought that some warning should be given. Oppenheimer now invited the scientific advisory panel to meet informally at Los Alamos. On June 9th they concluded: "We can propose no technical demonstration likely to bring an end to the war; we can see no acceptable alternative to direct military use (119)." *Choice of target*

Arthur Compton wrote later: "Our hearts were heavy as on June 16th we turned in this report to the Interim Committee (120)." The four scientists were fully aware of the doubts of some of their colleagues. They did not actually see the memorandum which James Franck and Leo Szilard were drafting early in June; but they knew of their increasing doubts about the use of the bomb.

The memorandum declared: "Nuclear bombs cannot possibly remain a 'secret weapon' at the exclusive disposal of this country for more than a few years . . . the United States, with its agglomeration of population and industry in comparatively few metropolitan districts, will be at a disadvantage compared to nations whose populations are scattered over large areas. We believe that these considerations make the use of nuclear bombs for an early unannounced attack against Japan inadvisable. If the United States were to be the first to release this new means of indiscriminate destruction upon mankind, we would sacrifice public support throughout the world, precipitate the race for armaments, and prejudice the possibility of reaching an international agreement on the future control of such weapons. Much more favourable conditions for the eventual achievement of such an agreement could be created if nuclear bombs were first to be revealed to the world by a *Franck Report*

61

demonstration in an appropriately selected and uninhabited area (121)."

The Franck Report was handed to Stimson on June 11th. The Interim Committee was not given a chance to study it. However, by the time the scientific advisory panel had reported, Karl Compton had gone over it with Franck. Thus the advice of the two groups of scientists were known to the Committee when they came to their conclusion: "The opinions of our scientific colleagues on the initial use of these weapons are not unanimous. They range from the proposal of a purely technical demonstration to that of the military application best designed to induce surrender . . . We find ourselves closer to these latter views (122)."

Oppenheimer wrote: "We didn't know beans about the military situation in Japan. We didn't know whether they could be caused to surrender by other means or whether the invasion was really inevitable . . . We thought the two overriding considerations were the saving of lives in the war and the effect of our actions on the stability of the postwar world. We did say that we did not think exploding one of these things as a firecracker over a desert was likely to be very impressive. This was before we had actually done that (123)."

The New Mexico test showed that such a demonstration could in fact be very impressive. True, the crater in the desert gave little idea of what the blast and radiation might do to a living city. Yet all who watched the test had been amazed. At this point the four scientists might have reconsidered their advice, and opted merely for a demonstration.

They might also have noted a poll which Compton took among his Chicago scientists. This poll offered a choice between five ways of using the bomb. Most of the Chicago men called for a military target, choosing "a military demonstration in Japan to be followed by renewed opportunity for surrender before full use of the weapon is employed (124)." But neither this poll, nor the test, made Oppenheimer and his three colleagues change their minds. In any case, it was too late for them to alter the Interim Committee's advice to the President. The decision in principle to use the bomb without warning had been taken.

At this point, formal British agreement was needed under the

Quebec Agreement. Sir John Anderson had been told two months *Britain follows*
ago: "The Americans propose to drop a bomb ... Do we agree that *America's lead*
the weapon should be used against the Japanese? If for any reason
we did not, the matter would presumably have to be raised by the
Prime Minister with the President. If we do agree, various points
still arise on which it would be desirable to have consultation with
the Americans . . . whether any warning should be given to the
Japanese (125)."

But Churchill never raised these questions with President Truman.
He accepted that the decision would really belong to America. The
Pacific, where the bomb would be used, was the American field of
action; and the Americans, despite the Maud Report and the
presence of British scientists at Los Alamos, had taken over the
whole project. Churchill agreed with Anderson to note the decision
at the next meeting of the Combined Policy Committee. On July
4th, "The Committee took note that the governments of the United
Kingdom and the United States had agreed that Tube Alloy
weapons should be used by the United States against Japan (126)."

The long term arguments of the Franck-Szilard report—and its
moral implications—were of slight interest to the politicians. Nor,
as some people have claimed, were the politicians under financial
pressure. They would certainly have liked to justify the two billion
dollars spent on the Manhattan project by the time Truman became
President. At Los Alamos it was believed that Congress would hold
an enquiry if the project should fail. When General Groves told his
assistants that he hoped to make a bomb by August, 1945, he added:
"If this weapon fizzles, each of you can look forward to a lifetime
of testifying before congressional investigating committees (127)."
But the Interim Committee was not responsible for Manhattan,
and so was under no financial pressure.

Nor were the scientists on the advisory panel influenced by *Scientists'*
budgeting. They naturally wanted to prove the success of their work. *motives*
As Robert Oppenheimer said, "When you see something that is tech-
nically sweet you go ahead and do it, and you argue about what to
do about it only after you have had your technical success. That is
the way it was with the atomic bomb (128)." Admiral Leahy
remarked that "the scientists and others wanted to make this test
because of the vast sums that had been spent on the project (129)."

But their success had already been proved in New Mexico. A repetition in Japan was unnecessary.

American strategy
The decision recorded on July 4th was strategic. Secretary of War Stimson had told the Interim Committee that their great task was to secure victory. The "objective of the United States in the summer of 1945 was the prompt and complete surrender of Japan . . . There was as yet no indication of any weakening in the Japanese determination to fight rather than accept unconditional surrender. If she could persist in her fight to the end, she still had a great military force. As we understood it in July, there was a very strong possibility that the Japanese government might determine upon resistance to the end (130)."

Bombing of Japan
How could Japan be defeated? General ("Hap") Arnold was convinced that conventional bombing, plus a naval blockade, would win the day. The Japanese surely could not endure more great "fire raids" such as Tokyo had suffered at the end of May? On the other hand, an intelligence report told Stimson early in July that, while "the Japanese economic position has deteriorated greatly, increasingly heavy air attacks, supplementing continued and intensified blockade, are seriously reducing Japan's production . . . The Japanese believe that unconditional surrender would be the equivalent of national extinction. There are as yet no indications that the Japanese are ready to accept such terms (131)." The report advocated that heavy bombing should be followed by an invasion of the Japanese mainland.

Invasion project
General Marshall believed that an invasion would succeed if Russia helped with an attack launched from Siberia. He told President Truman that "it might cost one half million lives to force the enemy's surrender on his home grounds (132)." Secretary Stimson thought the figure over-optimistic and the price too high. He advised Truman: "There is reason to believe that the operation for the occupation of Japan following the landing may be a very long, costly and arduous struggle on our part. The terrain . . . would be susceptible to a last ditch defence such as has been made on Iwo Jima and Okinawa . . . If we once land on one of the main islands and begin a forceful occupation of Japan we shall probably have cast the die of last ditch resistance. The Japanese are highly patriotic, and certainly susceptible to calls for fanatical resistance

to repel an invasion (133)." But contingency plans were still made for a landing in the south in November and on the Tokyo plain next spring.

Stimson had talked of "fanatical resistance." The bravery of the Japanese suicide pilots in their Kamikaze planes had already caused heavy losses of American men and ships. In the Okinawa campaign they had sunk 16 ships and damaged 185 more. They would have made invasion terribly costly. A journalist wrote that, "Although 2,500 Kamikaze planes had been expended, there were 5,350 of them still left and 7,000 under repair or in storage; and 5,000 young men were training for the Kamikaze corps (134)."

Neither bombing nor invasion, it seemed, would end the war swiftly. Might the Japanese agree to negotiate? It was known that a peace party led by the Foreign Minister, Togo, existed within the Tokyo government. The Emperor lent his ear to this party. Its members decided at a meeting in June: "Although we have no choice but to continue the war so long as the enemy insists upon unconditional surrender, we deem it advisable while we still possess considerable power of resistance, to propose peace through neutral powers (135)." The Japanese approached the Russians—still ostensibly neutral—and asked them to act as intermediaries with the Allies. *Japanese peace party*

The Japanese peace party was offering talks, not surrender. Japan had five million men in the field, a mainland free of enemy troops, and a fanatic patriotism. She was unlikely to accept the forcible occupation, change of government and disarmament implied by unconditional surrender.

Perhaps she would heed a powerful warning. Stimson told Truman: "I am inclined to think that there is enough such chance to make it well worth while our giving them a warning of what is to come and a definite opportunity to capitulate . . . Japan is not a nation composed wholly of mad fanatics . . . I think the Japanese nation has the mental intelligence to recognize the folly of a fight to the finish and to accept the proffer of what will amount to an unconditional surrender. It is therefore my conclusion that a carefully timed warning be given to Japan . . . *Stimson: warn Japan*

"Success of course will depend on the potency of the warning which we give her. This warning should contain . . . the varied and overwhelming character of the force we are about to bring to bear on the islands, the inevitability and completeness of the destruction which the full application of this force will entail . . . I personally think that if in saying this . . . we do not exclude a constitutional monarchy under her present dynasty, it would substantially add to the chance of acceptance (136)." In adding this rider, Stimson recognized the intensely loyal and semi-religious attachment of the Japanese to their Emperor.

Within a week of receiving this note from his Secretary for War, Truman left for the victory conference of the Allied powers at Potsdam. There he received a telegram telling him of the successful New Mexico test: "Operated on this morning. Diagnosis not yet complete but results seem satisfactory and already exceed expectations." The next day came another: "Dr. Groves has just returned most enthusiastic and confident that the little boy is as husky as his big brother (137)."

Churchill's reaction to Mexico test bomb

Churchill was at once told about the New Mexico test. He recalled: "In the afternoon Stimson called at my abode and laid before me a sheet of paper on which was written 'Babies satisfactorily born' (138)." An official present at the meeting reported Churchill's reaction: "Stimson, what was gunpowder? Trivial. What was electricity? Meaningless. The atomic bomb is the second coming in wrath (139)." Churchill himself described his feelings, and his dread of the necessary invasion of Japan: ". . . for we were resolved to share the agony. Now all this nightmare had vanished. In its place was the vision—fair and bright it seemed—of the end of the whole war in one or two violent shocks . . . Moreover, we should not need the Russians (140)."

In Potsdam on 23rd July General Sir Alan Brooke lunched with Churchill: "He had seen the American reports of results of the new Tube Alloys secret explosive. He was completely carried away. It was now no longer necessary for the Russians to come into the Japanese war; the new explosive alone was enough to settle the matter (141)."

Relations with the Russians had grown worse. Stalin had failed to help the Polish resistance in Warsaw, and had aroused suspicions at the Allied conference at Yalta in February. The invasion of Japan would require the help of Russian troops from the east, as General

Prime Minister Clement Attlee, President Truman and Marshal Stalin at
the Potsdam Conference (July, 1945) where Truman told Stalin about the
atom bomb

Marshall had made clear. Russia had promised to enter the war
within three months of Germany's surrender. If she did, she would
no doubt lay claim after the victory to Manchuria and extend her
influence in eastern Europe. Byrnes spoke for many Americans
when he wrote: "I must frankly admit that, in view of what we knew
of Soviet actions in eastern Germany and the violations of the Yalta
agreements . . . I would have been satisfied had the Russians
determined *not* to enter the war (142)."

If the war could be ended swiftly other than by invasion, Russia's
chance would be lost. But neither Churchill nor Truman wanted to
use the bomb primarily to keep Russia out of the war. Russian
neutrality would just be an added bonus.

The question now facing America and Britain was how much—if
anything—to tell Stalin about the bomb? Churchill reported to his
Cabinet: "The President . . . asked what I thought should be done

*Keeping Stalin
in the dark*

about telling the Russians. He seemed determined to do this, but asked about the timing, and said he thought that the end of the Conference would be best. I replied that if he were resolved to tell, it might well be better to hang it on the experiment, which was a new fact on which he had only just had knowledge . . . (143)."

A few days later Truman accosted Stalin at the end of a meeting: "On July 24th I casually mentioned to Stalin that we had a new weapon of special destructive force. The Russian Premier showed no unusual interest. All he said was that he was glad to hear it and hoped we would make 'good use of it against the Japanese' (144)." Churchill, who watched Stalin's face across the room, wrote a more vivid account of the exchange: "He seemed to be delighted. A new bomb! Of extraordinary power! Probably decisive in the whole Japanese war! What a bit of luck! This was my impression of the moment, and I was sure that he had no idea of the significance of what he was being told (145)."

Churchill's impression was probably wrong. Since the spring, Communist agents had been giving Moscow reports of the Manhattan project slipped to them by Klaus Fuchs in Los Alamos, and by Pontecorvo and Nunn May in Canada. We do not know how seriously the Russian scientists took these reports, or to whom they had passed them. But perhaps they explained Stalin's indifference on hearing President Truman's news.

Truman wrote in his memoirs that after hearing of the Mexico test, "I then agreed to the use of the atomic bomb if Japan did not yield (146)." The Japanese war party seemed to be in the ascendant. James Byrnes recalled: "We faced a terrible decision. We could not rely on Japan's inquiries to the Soviet Union about a negotiated peace as proof that Japan would surrender unconditionally without the use of the bomb. In fact, Stalin stated the last message to him had said that Japan would 'fight to the death rather than accept unconditional surrender.' Under these circumstances, agreement to negotiate could only arouse false hopes. Instead, we relied upon the Potsdam Declaration (147)."

Truman's ultimatum to Japan

America decided to warn Japan rather as suggested by Stimson. The Japanese were told that the leaders of the United States, Great Britain and China "have conferred and agreed that Japan shall be given an opportunity to end the war . . . The following are our terms.

We shall not deviate from them. There are no alternatives. We shall brook no delay . . . Japanese sovereignty shall be limited to the islands of Honshu, Hokkaido, Kyushu, Shikoku and such minor islands as we determine. The Japanese military forces, after being completely disarmed, shall be permitted to return to their homes . . . We do not intend that the Japanese shall be enslaved as a race nor destroyed as a nation . . . The occupying forces of the Allies shall be withdrawn as soon as . . . there has been established, in accordance with the freely expressed will of the Japanese people, a peacefully inclined and responsible government. We call upon the Government of Japan to proclaim now the unconditional surrender of all the Japanese armed forces . . . The alternative for Japan is complete and utter destruction (148)."

This was a milder version of the warning advocated by Stimson. Stimson had stressed that the success of any warning would depend on its potency. The vague threat of "complete and utter destruction" hardly matched the "overwhelming character of the force" about to be unleashed. Also, the declaration was ambiguous as to the future of the Emperor. The "peacefully inclined and responsible government" was hardly the "present dynasty" which Stimson had in mind. Admiral Leahy commented later: "It was noteworthy that the message contained no hint of the projected employment against the Japanese of our recently completed atom bomb (149)."

The peace party in the Japanese War Council was still trying to negotiate through the Russians. But Truman's ultimatum ended their hope that any talks might be acceptable. The war party persuaded the aged Prime Minister Suzuki to reject the ultimatum. Byrnes wrote: "We devoutly hoped that the Japanese would heed our warning that, unless they surrendered unconditionally, the destruction of their armed forces and the devastation of their homeland was inevitable. But, on July 28th, the Japanese Premier issued a statement saying the declaration was unworthy of notice. That was disheartening. There was nothing left to do but use the bomb (150)." *Japan fights on*

A week earlier Truman had received more cables from home: "Patient progressing rapidly and will be ready for final operation first good break August." And then, "Operation may be possible any time from August 1st depending on state of preparation of patient and condition of atmosphere (151)." He had at once told *Timing the attack*

69

the War Department to order the Commanding General of the United States Army, General Spaatz, to drop the bomb as soon as possible after August 3rd.

Truman was later asked why he had given this order *before* the ultimatum had been sent to Japan. He replied: "I ordered atomic bombs dropped on the two cities named on the way back from Potsdam when we were in the middle of the Atlantic Ocean. In your letter, you raise the fact that the directive to General Spaatz to prepare for delivering the bomb is dated July 25th. It was, of course, necessary to set the military wheels in motion, as these orders did, but the final decision was in my hands and was not made until I was returning from Potsdam (152)."

Aboard the *Augusta*, in mid-Atlantic, Truman confirmed the order to Spaatz.

6 *Hiroshima Holocaust*

Truman's bombing order

TRUMAN'S ORDER of July 25th, confirmed on his way home from Potsdam, instructed General Spaatz: "The 509th Composite Group, 20th Air Force, will deliver its special bomb as soon as weather will permit visual bombing after 3rd August, 1945, on one of the targets: Hiroshima, Kokura, Niigata and Nagasaki. To carry military and civilian scientific personnel from the War Department to observe and record the effects of the explosion of the bomb, additional aircraft will accompany the airplane carrying the bomb . . . Additional bombs will be delivered on the above targets as soon as made ready by the project staff (153)."

The list of cities had been drawn up earlier in the month. Truman recalled, 'Stimson's staff had prepared a list of cities in Japan that might serve as targets. Kyoto, though favoured by General Arnold as a centre of military activity, was eliminated when Secretary Stimson pointed out that it was a cultural and religious shrine of the Japanese (154)."

Final briefings

The confirmation of Truman's order was flashed to the island base of Tinian, where General Farrell was deputizing for Groves. Farrell struck Niigata off the list of possible targets: it was too far away. On August 2nd the last batch of components for the bomb arrived on the island. The final decision concerned the weather. The forecasters announced that the skies would clear on August 5th.

The pilots were briefed: "You will proceed to a rendezvous at Iwo with two other B.29s. Only one plane will carry it. The other planes will carry instruments and photographic equipment. You three will not contact each other, but will maintain the strictest radio silence. Weather observation planes . . . will not address you directly, but speak as if addressing the base at Tinian . . . You will approach the target at a ground speed around 300 m.p.h. Bombing will be visual. If the city of choice is not clear, proceed at your discretion to another target. As bomb is released, you will immediately turn at a 150-degree angle. You must not—repeat *not*—follow standard bombing procedure by proceeding as usual to fly over the target (155)."

Next evening, Colonel Tibbets addressed the pilots who were to fly with him in the three bombers: "Tonight is the night we have all been waiting for. Our long months of training are to be put to the test. We will soon know if we have been successful or failed. Upon our efforts tonight it is possible that history will be made. We are going on a mission to drop a bomb different from any you have ever seen or heard about. This bomb contains a destructive force equivalent to 20,000 tons of T.N.T. (156)." So well had the secret been kept that even the air crews did not know what kind of bomb was loaded in the *Enola Gay* (one of the planes). They were now told of the expected blast effect. But they were still not told of the radiation risk which made it so vital that they should not fly over the explosion.

Barnard's ballad
Three weather planes took off soon after midnight. Then the three B.29s carrying the bomb, measuring instruments, and cameras followed. Sergeant Harry Barnard wrote a ballad (157):

> *It was the 6th of August, that much we knew*
> *When the boys took off in the morning dew.*
> *Feeling nervous, sick and ill at ease*
> *They flew at the heart of the Japanese.*

The bomb run
In the *Enola Gay* with Tibbets were the explosive expert Parsons, and Captain Lewis. Parsons had decided that, in view of the danger of a take-off accident, the final assembly of the bomb should be carried out on board. Captain Lewis kept a log of the flight: "At forty five minutes out of our base everyone is at work . . . I think everyone will feel relieved when we have left our bomb with the Japs . . . It is 5.05 and we are only a few miles from Iwo Jima . . . At 7.30 Captain Parsons has put the final touches on his assembly job. We are now loaded. The bomb is now alive. It is a funny feeling knowing it is right in back of you. Knock wood.

"We started our second climb to our final altitude at 7.40 . . . We have now set the automatic pilot for the last time until 'bombs away' . . . At 8.30 we received a report from the weather plane that our primary is the best target, so . . . we will make a bomb run on Hiroshima right now . . . We are now only 25 miles from the Empire, and everyone has a big hopeful look on his face. It is 8.50. Not long now, folks . . . the Colonel [Tibbets] and I are standing by and giving the boys what they want . . . There will be a short intermission while we bomb our target . . . My God! (158)"

The great bomb plummetted from the sky. Back on Tinian, Parsons took up Lewis's story: "It was at 9.15 when we dropped our bomb, and we turned the plane broadside to get the best view . . . It was a terrific spectacle. The base of the lower part of the mushroom, a mass of purplish-grey dust about three miles in diameter, was all boiling . . . The mushroom top was also boiling, a seething turbulent mass. The mushroom smoke reached our altitude. Then another mushroom came up, also very turbulent . . . It looked as though it was coming from a huge burning fire, and seemed to settle back to earth again. The purple clouds and flames were whirling around. It seemed as though the whole town got pulverized (159)." *The mushroom cloud*

At 9.30 a.m. Tibbets wired to Tinian island: "Mission successful." When at last he stepped down onto the runway from the *Enola Gay*, General Spaatz pinned the Distinguished Service Cross to his jacket. He read the citation: "Flying a B.29 on a daring day strike on Hiroshima, carrying for the first time a bomb totally new to modern warfare, he successfully dropped his bomb upon reaching the target city . . . the culmination of many months of tireless effort, training and organization unique in American Air Force history, during which he constantly coped with new problems in precision bombing and engineering (160)."

Later in the day, General Farrell collated the descriptions of the pilots. Then he sent a report to General Groves: "First there was a ball of fire changing in a few seconds to purple clouds and flames boiling and swirling upward. Flash observed just after airplane rolled out of turn. All agreed light was intensely bright. Entire city except outermost ends of dock areas was covered with a dark gray dust layer which joined the cloud column. It was extremely turbulent with flashes of fire visible in the dust. Estimated diameter of this *Farrell's report*

General Spaatz pinning the Distinguished Service Cross to Colonel
Tibbet's jacket after the successful bombing of Hiroshima

Opposite: Atomic "fungus" seen over Hiroshima after the explosion

dust layer is at least three miles. One observer stated it looked as though whole town was being torn apart (161)."

*   *   *

AS HIROSHIMA had been spared the fire-bomb raids suffered by other Japanese cities, local talk had it that the Allies might be planning a special attack against her. Some townsfolk had evacuated. But 40,000 Japanese troops had recently been stationed in the already densely populated city. The only precaution taken by the Hiroshima authorities had been to demolish houses to make clearways to stop fires spreading. At seven o'clock on the morning of August 6th, the siren sounded. At eight it was followed by the all clear. The people of Hiroshima began their day.

A lucky survivor

The Reverend Tanimoto was moving furniture from his church to a safe area outside Hiroshima. He had just arrived at a friend's house in the surrounding foothills: "Then a tremendous flash of light cut across the sky . . . It seemed a sheet of sun. He threw himself between two high rocks in the garden. He felt a sudden pressure and then splinters and pieces of board and fragments of tile fell on top of him. When he dared he raised his head and saw that the house had collapsed. He thought a bomb had fallen directly on it. Such clouds of dust had risen that there was a sort of twilight around. In panic he dashed out into the street. He noticed that the concrete wall of the estate had fallen over. Under what seemed to be a local dust cloud the day grew darker and darker (162)."

A doctor's diary

Nearer the middle of the town the victims were not only subject to blast. Dr. Hachiya of the Hiroshima Communications Hospital recalled: "The hour was early, the morning still. Clad in vest and pants I was sprawled on the living room floor exhausted, because I had spent a sleepless night on duty as an air raid warden in my hospital. Suddenly a strong flash of light startled me—and then another . . . The garden became brilliantly lit, and I debated whether this light was caused by a magnesium flare or sparks from a passing tram. Garden shadows disappeared. The view where a moment before all had been so bright and sunny was now dark and hazy. Through swirling dust I could barely discern a wooden column that had supported one corner of my house. It was leaning crazily, and the roof sagged dangerously . . . I tried to escape but rubble and fallen timbers barred the way . . . A profound weakness overcame

A view of the devastation left after the explosion of the atomic bomb
over Hiroshima

me. To my surprise I discovered that I was completely naked. How
odd! Where were my vest and pants? What had happened? All over
the right side of my body I was cut and bleeding (163)."

Few survived in the middle of Hiroshima near the explosion. *Burned people*
When Tanimoto went into the town to seek his family, he "tried at
several points to penetrate the ruins, but the flames always stopped
him. Under many houses people screamed for help, but no one
helped . . . the wounded limped past the screams and Mr. Tanimoto
ran past them . . . all the way he overtook dreadfully burned and
lacerated people. As much of Hiroshima as he could see through
the clouded air was giving off a thick, dreadful miasma. Clumps of
smoke had begun to push up through the general dust. He wondered
how such extensive damage could have been dealt out of a silent
sky . . . Houses nearby were burning (164)." New fires were leaping
up and swiftly spreading.

A friend told Dr. Hachiya a few days later how, "Hundreds of *Fire and water*
people sought refuge in the Asana Park. They had refuge from the

approaching flames for a little while, but gradually the fire forced them nearer the river until at length everyone was crowded on to the steep bank overlooking the river . . . Even though the river is more than 100 metres wide along the border of the park, balls of fire were being carried through the air from the opposite shore and soon the pine trees in the park were afire. The poor people faced a fiery death if they stayed in the park and a watery death if they jumped in the river. I could hear shouting and crying and in a few minutes they began to fall like toppling dominoes into the river (165)."

The fires were not the only hazard. "It began to rain. The drops grew abnormally large, and someone shouted: 'The Americans are dropping gasoline! They're going to set fire to us!' But the drops were

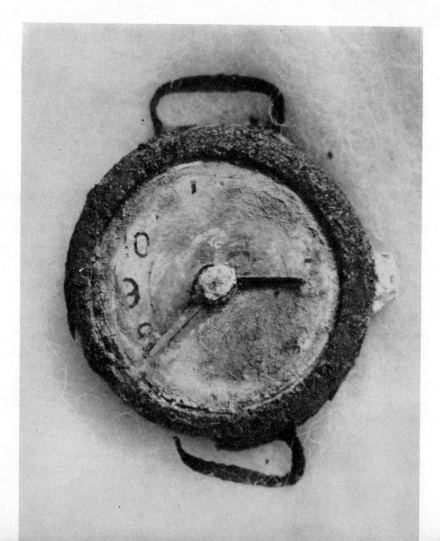

water, and as they fell the wind grew stronger and stronger—and suddenly a whirlwind ripped through the park. Huge trees crashed down; small ones were uprooted and flew into the air. Higher, a wild array of flat things revolved in the twisting funnel—pieces of iron roofing, doors, strips of matting (166)." The pebble-sized raindrops were drops of condensed moisture falling from the cloud of dust and fission fragments.

By the time Tanimoto reached Asana Park, "It was very crowded, and to distinguish the living from the dead was not easy, for most of the people lay still with their eyes open . . . The burned ones were quiet. No one wept, much less screamed in pain. No one complained. None of the many who died did so noisily." On a long sandspit by the river he "found about twenty men and women . . . They did not move and he realized that they were too weak to lift themselves. He reached down and took a woman by the hands, but her skin slipped off in huge glove-like pieces. He was so sickened by this that he had to sit down a minute . . . He remembered uneasily what the great burns he had seen during the day had been like: yellow at first, then red and swollen, with the skin sloughed off and finally, in the evening, suppurated and smelly (167)."

Skinned alive

The luckier ones managed to drag themselves to the hospitals for the little shelter they could still offer. After his house had collapsed on him, Dr. Hachiya found himself in one of his own wards: "I must have slept soundly . . . The groans of patients assaulted my ears. Everything was in turmoil . . . instruments, window frames and debris littered the floor . . . An old friend came in. His face and hands were burned. I asked him if he knew what had happened. He answered, 'The first thing I knew there was a blinding white flash and a wave of intense heat struck my cheek . . . Hundreds of injured people who were trying to escape to the hills passed our house. Their faces and hands were burned and swollen; and great sheets of skin had peeled away from their tissues to hang down like rags on a scarecrow. They moved like a line of ants. All through the night they went past our house, but this morning they had stopped. I found them lying on both sides of the road so thick that it was impossible to pass without stepping on them' (168)."

Hospitals

Another man in the hospital told Dr. Hachiya: "I walked along the railway tracks to get here, but even they were littered with

79

Opposite: The hands on the watch show the actual time the atomic bomb hit Hiroshima: 8.15 a.m.

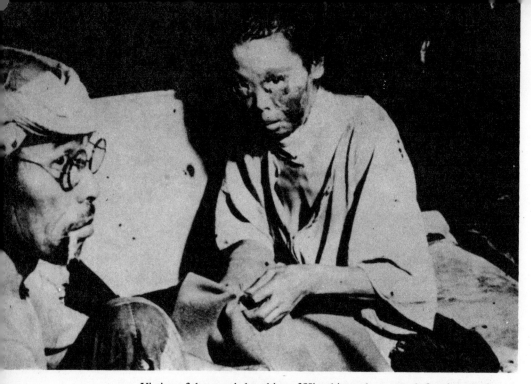

Victims of the atomic bombing of Hiroshima: the woman's face is severely scarred by the tremendous heat that the explosion generated

electric wires and broken railway cars, and the dead and wounded lay everywhere. When I reached the bridge I saw a man, stone dead, sitting on his bicycle as it leaned against the bridge railing. It is hard to believe that such a thing could happen . . . It seems that most of the dead people were either on the bridge or beneath it. You could tell that many had gone down to the river to get a drink of water and had died where they lay. I saw a few live people still in the water, knocking against the dead as they floated down the river. There must have been hundreds and thousands who fled to the river to escape the fire and then drowned.

"The sight of the soldiers, though, was more dreadful than the dead people floating down the river. I came on I don't know how many, burned from the hips up, and where the skin had peeled, their flesh was wet and mushy . . . And they had no faces! Their eyes, noses and mouths had been burned away and it looked like their ears had melted off. It was hard to tell front from back. One soldier, whose features had been destroyed and was left with his white teeth sticking out, asked me for some water but I didn't have any (169)."

A broken city   The bridge of Hiroshima where so many died was ruined. When

Dr. Hachiya was well enough to go out into the town from the hospital he saw that the bridge "was so buckled that its reinforced concrete surface had been thrown into waves. It was so cracked and shattered that gaping holes exposed the river below . . . Below the bridge on the east bank of the river had stood the bronze domed Museum of Science and Industry . . . Its bronze dome was gone, its sturdy walls of brick and stone cracked and crumbled and its interior devoured by fire (170)." It was later deduced from the scorchings on telegraph poles, and the prints of shadows caused by the initial flash, that the bomb had fallen about fifty yards southeast of the bridge. At this point the pillars of the Shima Hospital were driven straight into the ground.

The *New York Times* stated: "Japanese newspapers featured an aerial photograph of atom-bombed Hiroshima showing 'the city completely reduced to ashes and only one chimney standing upright (171)." A clergyman, Father Kleinsorge, later told how the "naked trees and canted telephone poles, the few standing, gutted buildings only accentuated the horizontality of everything else . . . and in the streets a macabre traffic—hundreds of crumpled bicycles, shells of street cars and automobiles, all halted in mid-motion (172)."

Dr. Hachiya found that "the tram wire and its supporting cables were down, so about every fifty feet we had to crawl over or under a cable . . . Other obstacles were fallen poles and toppling walls . . . There were tile walls and broken tubs to distinguish the homes that had once had bathrooms . . . Many of the inhabitants I had known, but the place was so strange to me now that for the life of me I could not have said where any of them had lived (173)."

People could not recognize their own homes. Some of those who had crawled out of the city returned hungry for rice. "At first when they got among the rows of prostrate houses they did not know where they were; the change was too sudden. From a busy city of 245,000 that morning to a mere pattern of residue in the afternoon. The asphalt of the streets was still so soft and hot from the fires that walking was uncomfortable. They encountered only one person, a woman, who said to them as they passed, 'My husband is in those ashes' (174)."

That first day Hiroshima was deserted. Anyone who could had crawled to the hospitals. Sixty-five of the city's doctors were dead,

Hiroshima's atomic bomb damage: *above* the remains of a church and *below* a temporary first-aid station

many more injured. Of 2,400 nurses, 1,800 had been killed or injured. Dr. Sasaki, the only unharmed doctor on the staff of the Red Cross Hospital, grabbed bandages, "went out into the corridor, and began patching up the wounded patients and the doctors and nurses there . . . worked without method, taking those who were nearest to him first; and he noticed soon that the corridor seemed to be getting more and more crowded. Mixed in with the abrasions and lacerations which most people had suffered he began to find dreadful burns. He realized then that casualties were pouring in from outdoors. There were so many that he began to pass up the lightly wounded; he decided that all he could hope to do was to stop people from bleeding to death.

"Before long, patients lay and crouched on the floors of the wards and the laboratories and all the other rooms and in the corridors and on the stairs and in the front hall and on the stone front steps . . . and in the driveway and courtyard and for blocks each way in the streets outside. Wounded people supported maimed people. Disfigured families leaned together. Many were vomiting. A tremendous number of schoolgirls—who had been taken from their classrooms to work clearing fire lanes—crept into the hospital . . . The people in the suffocating crowd inside the hospital wept and cried and the less seriously injured came and pulled at his sleeve and begged him to come to the aid of the worse wounded (175)."

The ghastly burns marked almost all the victims. The burns were mysterious. Dr. Fujii had noticed as he watched the wounded people filing past him that "although there were as yet very few fires . . . many of them exhibited terrible burns on their faces and arms (176)." The burns were caused not by the fires but by the neutrons, beta particles, and gamma rays released when the bomb exploded. This radiation, combined with the blast, had killed nearly everyone within half a mile of the explosion and many thousands further away. As Dr. Sasaki said, "The doctors realized in retrospect that even though most of these dead had also suffered from burns and blast effects, they had absorbed enough radiation to kill them. The rays simply destroyed body cells—caused their nuclei to degenerate and broke their walls (177)."

Radiation burns

Many died within a few days after horrible vomiting and diarrhoea. About a fortnight after the explosion a new symptom

Radiation sickness

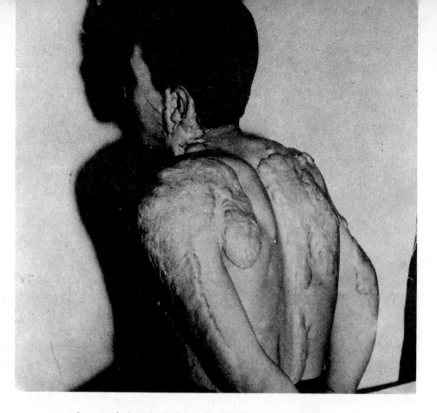

An atomic bomb victim suffering from severe burns

appeared. Mrs. Nakamura, for example, had been knocked over by the blast three quarters of a mile from the explosion, but had suffered no cuts or burns. "As she dressed on the morning of August 20th she began fixing her hair and noticed, after one stroke, that her comb carried with it a whole handful of hair; the second time, the same thing happened . . . In the next three or four days her hair kept falling out of its own accord, until she was quite bald. She began living indoors, practically in hiding. She woke up on August 26th feeling extremely weak and tired (178)."

Many hospital inmates, too, began to lose their hair. Doctors and patients alike became increasingly nervous. Dr. Hachiya grabbed some of his own hair and pulled: "I did not have much hair in the first place, but the amount that came out made me feel sick (179)."

He and the other doctors watched in horror the progress of this "radiation sickness": "We thought that by giving treatment to those who were burned or injured, recovery would follow. But now it was obvious that this was not true. People who appeared to be recovering developed other symptoms that caused them to die. So many

"Shadows" cast by a bridge hand-rail give a clear definition of the direction of the explosion over Hiroshima

patients died without our understanding the cause of death that we were all in despair. They all had symptoms which we could not explain, and during the past few days spots had begun to appear. These were cause for greater alarm . . . They bore no relationship to the type or severity of injury, and those who appeared to be un-injured—and had even felt well enough to help in the care of other patients—were beginning to show these blood spots beneath the skin. Presumably healthy people developed petechiae and died (180)."

As these boils or "petechiae" appeared, fevers rose and blood counts fell. Dr. Hachiya found that "the patients were suffering from a blood disease characterized by a suppression of the white blood cells (181)." Despite his own growing weariness, despite the difficulties of working in the ruined hospital and the shortage of equipment and food, he found time and energy to study the symptoms of the patients. He also recorded their exact positions at the time of the explosion: "In general I found those closest to the hypocentre [point where the bomb fell] to have the severest symp-

toms, and the greater the distance the fewer and milder the symptoms. There were, however, a few exceptions. Some patients quite near the hypocentre had minimal symptoms and a nearly normal white count. By studying these cases individually I found the reason. These patients had been shielded by reinforced concrete buildings, large trees or other barriers (182)."

Hiroshima's death toll mounted. Hachiya wrote: "People were dying so fast that I had begun to accept death as a matter of course, and ceased to respect its awfulness. I considered a family lucky if it had not lost more than two of its members (183)." Father Siemes, a clergyman working among the dying, later told a journalist: "Official statistics place the number who died at 70,000 up to September 1st, not counting the missing and the 130,000 wounded. Estimates made by ourselves on the basis of groups known to us show that the number of 100,000 dead is not too high (184)."

In February, 1946, Supreme Allied Headquarters announced that the casualties in Hiroshima as a result of the atomic bomb were: dead 78,150, still missing 13,983, seriously wounded 9,428, slightly injured 27,997. Half the victims had died from the blast of the explosion, thirty per cent from radiation burns and the rest from other radiation effects (185).

86

Above: Young children in atom-blasted Hiroshima wearing masks over their noses and mouths to combat the odour of death around them

7 Nagasaki

ON BOARD the *Augusta* President Truman received a cable from the island of Tinian: "Big bomb dropped on Hiroshima . . . First reports indicate complete success which was even more conspicuous than earlier test (186)." Admiral Leahy, who was also on board, recalled: "A few minutes before noon, while the President was eating lunch with the crew, Captain Frank Graham . . . handed him a brief message from the Navy Department which bore the highest priority marks . . . Truman was excited over the news. He shook Captain Graham's hand and said, 'This is the greatest thing in history.' He then came back to the table and signalled the assembled crew in the mess hall that he wished to say something . . . The crew cheered as Truman finished his brief announcement (187)."

News of Hiroshima

The Presidential statement, prepared before Truman had left for the Potsdam conference, was immediately released from Washington: "It is an atomic bomb. It is a harnessing of the basic power of the universe. The force from which the sun draws its power has been loosed against those who brought war to the Far East . . . It was to spare the Japanese people from utter destruction that the ultimatum of July 26th was issued at Potsdam. Their leaders promptly rejected that ultimatum. If they do not now accept our terms, they may expect a rain of ruin from the air, the like of which has never been seen on this earth (188)."

Anglo-American statements

Prime Minister Clement Attlee announced in London: "The problems of the release of energy by atomic fission have been solved, and an atomic bomb has been dropped on Japan by the United States Army Air Force (189)." Attlee then issued the statement about the new bomb which Churchill had drawn up before his unexpected electoral defeat in July, 1945. An early public opinion survey, Mass Observation, recorded British reactions. One woman told an interviewer: "I think it's marvellous. It's just what we want, isn't it?" But another interviewer heard a man tell his family that after the B.B.C. news bulletin, "I watched all your faces the whole time and I could see nothing but dismay. One would think that the Japs had invented it (190)."

John Lehmann, the writer, noted in his journal: "The explosion of the atom bomb over Japan has made me feel physically sick (191)." The journalist Kingsley Martin commented in the *New Statesman*: "The B.B.C. announcers have all adopted a tone of solemn jubilation in reading the news of the atomic bomb's success . . . I very much doubt whether this chimes with the mood of the public. Obviously, we are all relieved that the Germans didn't drop it on London, but apart from that, everyone I've met was plunged into gloom by the news of the invention. While we are told officially of 'excellent results,' I find everywhere an increasing moral revulsion (192)."

The London *Times* correspondent in Washington could find no "word or phrase which adequately describes American reactions to the news of the use of the atom bomb. Some people are jubilant; others are shocked; some are incredulous; and on the lips of many is the word 'awful' used in its original sense because they realize how terrible it could be in ruthless hands (193)." A long poem by an American poet caught the prevalent mood so well that it went into a dozen editions in a few months. One passage read (194):

When the bomb fell on America it fell on people.
It didn't dissolve them as it dissolved people in Hiroshima.
It did not dissolve their bodies.
But it dissolved something vitally important
To the greatest of them and the least.
What it dissolved were their links with the past and with the future . . .
It made the earth that seemed so solid, Main Street, that seemed so
well paved,
A kind of vast jelly, quivering and dividing underfoot . . .
What have we done, my country, what have we done?

The news was broadcast all over Europe. Otto Hahn, the scientist who had first split the atom in 1938, was badly shocked. One of his colleagues said: "I am very worried about Otto Hahn. This news has upset him dreadfully, and I fear the worst (195)."

The Japanese outside Hiroshima were the last to hear of the holocaust. Their government had never kept them fully informed of events. The War Council still wished to preserve the nation's will to fight. So the news bulletins and the press underplayed the attack. The Japanese Home Service announced early on the morning of August 7th: "A small number of B.29s penetrated into Hiroshima City a little after 8 a.m. yesterday morning and dropped a small number of bombs. As a result a considerable number of homes were reduced to ashes and fires broke out in various parts of the city (196)." Later in the day there was mention of a new type of bomb. The *Daily Mirror* told its British readers: "The first official communiqué on the bombing of Hiroshima showed complete ignorance of its nature. The communiqué told of 'considerable damage by new types of bombs', though only one was used, apparently because the destruction was so great that they could not believe one bomb had caused it (197)." *Japanese news*

But as well as reading their newspapers, the Japanese could see the three million American leaflets (translated by Japanese prisoners) dropped over the country by B.29s from Tinian. They were told: "We are in possession of the most destructive explosive ever devised by man. A single one of our newly developed atomic bombs is actually the equivalent in explosive power of what 2,000 of our B.29s can carry on a single mission. This awful fact is one for you to ponder . . . We have just begun to use this weapon against your homeland. If you still have any doubt, make inquiry as to what happened to Hiroshima when just one atomic bomb fell on that city. Before using this bomb to destroy every resource of the military by which they are prolonging this useless war, we ask that you now petition the Emperor to end the war . . . You should take steps now to cease military resistance (198)." *U.S.A. propaganda leaflets*

The Japanese War Council met on August 8th to decide whether or not to end the war. Foreign Minister Togo wanted surrender if only the Emperor could remain; the War Minister if occupation could be avoided. They were trying to reach a compromise acceptable *Japan hesitates* both to the Allies and to the Japanese people.

Meanwhile, the parts of the plutonium bomb "Fat Man" had arrived on Tinian. Truman's order of July 25th to General Spaatz had mentioned "additional bombs". It was left to General Farrell to decide when "Fat Man" should be dropped. Farrell's decision was made before "Little Boy" left Tinian in the aircraft *Enola Gay*. The official reporter who had hoped to fly on this first mission wrote later: "Immediately upon my arrival in Tinian I sought out General Farrell, hoping that there was still time to arrange for my going along. General Farrell told me that it was too late, but that I would go on the next mission which at that time was scheduled for August 11th (199)."

Before this date, the Americans could have judged the Japanese government's reaction to the first bomb and to the propaganda leaflets. But Farrell took advantage of a forecast of bad weather later in the week to bring forward the date. Orders went out for the second atomic raid on August 8th. They listed two targets: "Kokura Arsenal and City . . . Nagasaki Urban Area (200)." General Groves remembered: "Admiral Purnell and I had often discussed the importance of having the second blow follow the first one quickly, so that the Japanese would not have time to recover their balance. It was Purnell who had first advanced the belief that two bombs would end the war, so I knew that with him and Farrell on the ground at Tinian there would be no unnecessary delay in exploiting our first success (201)."

Nagasaki holocaust

On August 8th "Fat Man" was loaded into the B.29 called *Bock's Car*. Its 64 detonators were arranged in a circle for the implosion method of driving the pieces of plutonium into a critical mass. The detonators were primed before take-off. Thick cloud lay over Kokura; *Bock's Car* flew on to Nagasaki. The city could be seen through a gap in the cloud. Farrell had kept his promise to the journalist. From an escorting B.29 he described the scene:

"We heard the pre-arranged signal on our radio, put on our arc welders' glasses and watched tensely the manoeuvrings of the strike ship about half a mile in front of us . . . What looked like a black object went downward . . . Even though we were turning away in the opposite direction, and despite the fact that it was broad daylight in our cabin, all of us became aware of a giant flash that broke

Opposite: Smoke billowing out into a mushroom shape 20,000 feet above Nagasaki after the atomic raid

A view of Nagasaki after the atomic explosion

through the dark barrier of our lenses and flooded our cabin with intense light. After the first flash . . . the light lingered on, a bluish-green light that illuminated the entire sky all around. A tremendous blast wave struck our ship and made it tremble from nose to tail. This was followed by four more blasts in rapid succession . . . Observers in the tail of our ship saw a giant ball of fire rise as though

The power of the atomic blast over Nagasaki is shown by the effect on the trees half a mile away from the centre of damage

from the bowels of the earth, belching forth enormous white smoke rings. Next they saw a giant pillar of purple fire, 10,000 feet high, shooting skyward with enormous speed. By the time our ship had made another turn . . . the pillar of purple fire had reached the level of our altitude. Awestruck, we watched it shoot upward. Then . . . there came shooting out of the top a giant mushroom, seething and boiling in a white fury of creamy foam, sizzling upward and then descending . . . (202)."

A boy's nightmare Below, ten year old Makoto Nagai was taking a swim in the river just outside Nagasaki. Suddenly he saw an "awful light in the sky . . . I just dived head first into the water. When I came up, from down the river came a noise like thunder. It was a terrific rush of wind. The leaves were torn off all the trees and came racing along . . . It was getting dark and cold very fast. I thought an airplane must have crashed into the sun. I ran to the house . . . Everything was smashed . . . Over Mount Kawahura . . . the biggest thing I ever saw, the biggest thing that ever was, was sticking right up into the sky. It was like a cloud but it was like a pillar of fire too. The light it sent out was all the colours of the rainbow. It almost blinded me with the glare. It kept getting taller and taller all the time, and wider and wider. It was growing from the top. I mean, the top was getting pushed up from inside. Then the top began to spread out so that it looked like an umbrella opening up . . .

A city destroyed "After a few minutes I saw something coming up the road along the river that looked like a parade of roast chickens. Some of them kept asking for water. I ran back to the cottage. I would rather blind myself than ever have to see such a sight again (203)."

The boy Makoto was three miles away from the explosion. He rushed to take shelter: "At that instant there was a blinding light. It was a brilliant blue flame . . . I have no idea how long it was before I came to . . . I must have been hurled against the wall by the blast and knocked out. In the dim light coming through the mouth of the shelter I saw a huddle of half naked people stream about the entrance way. Their bodies were puffed up like balloons, their skin was peeling off in strips, hanging down like the shreds of a rag. They were so still I thought they were dead but they weren't; they kept moaning, 'Water, give me water!' (204)"

The survivors of Nagasaki, as in Hiroshima, suffered terribly from radiation sickness. The destruction of the city was complete. The *New York Times* carried the report of a correspondent who flew over the following day: "Nagasaki was still a mass of angry flames twelve hours after the bombing. It was like looking over the rim of a volcano in the process of eruption." The same issue reported: "General Carl Spaatz announced today that the atomic

The blast effect on a gas-holder, half a mile away from the centre of damage at Nagasaki

bombing of Nagasaki on Thursday destroyed thirty per cent of that city's sprawling industrial area, including the big Mitsubishi steel works and other heavy industries that played a major role in the Japanese war (205)." General Spaatz, according to the press report, "did not estimate how many thousands of Japanese might have been killed by the bomb." The figure was later put at 45,000. Some 25,000 others were injured.

The Japanese War Council were still arguing at their meeting with Emperor Hirohito when they heard the news of Nagasaki. *Japan surrenders* The previous night they had also heard that Russia had declared war on them, and that Russian troops were moving into Manchuria. Premier Suzuki told the Council early on the morning of the 10th: "Gentlemen, we have spent hours in deliberation without coming to a decision . . . You are fully aware that we cannot afford to waste even a minute at this juncture. I propose, therefore, to seek the Imperial guidance and substitute it for the decision of this conference

95

(206)." The Emperor told the Council that he must "call a halt to the war and accept the Allies' terms, bearing what was indeed very hard to bear (207)." These terms were embodied in the Allies' Potsdam Declaration.

Japan's acceptance of the Potsdam Declaration—on one condition, that the Emperor should be allowed to remain—was sent at once to Washington. Sir Alan Brooke wrote in his diary: "Just before lunch B.B.C. interceptions of Japanese peace offers were received in the shape of an acceptance of the Potsdam offer. There was, however, one rather obscure clause concerning the prerogatives of the Emperor being retained (208)." The American reply was ambiguous on the position of the Emperor. Hirohito himself wished to accept it, but the war party still wished to continue an all-out war.

Rebels in Japan

A military group even planned a *coup d'état* to oust the Emperor and the War Council. They bombed Foreign Minister Togo's house. Karl Compton wrote later: "It is not generally realized there was any threat of a revolt against the Government, led by an army group supported by the peasants, to seize control and continue the war. For several days it was touch and go whether the people would follow their government into surrender (209)."

But the armed rebellion came to nothing. The Emperor accepted Truman's terms and broadcast his decision to the Japanese people. In his Hiroshima hospital, Dr. Hachiya wrote: "Darkness clouded my eyes, my teeth chattered and I felt cold sweat running down my back . . . The ward was quiet and silence reigned for a long time . . . By degrees people began to whisper and then to talk. Expressions of anger were unleashed: 'Only a coward would back out now.' 'I would rather die than be defeated.' 'What have we been suffering for?' (210)"

But it was too late. Truman had received Japan's capitulation. He announced: "I deem this reply a full acceptance of the Potsdam Declaration which specified the unconditional surrender of Japan. In the reply there is no qualification (211)."

Were the bombs needed?

The Second World War was over at last. One military historian recently claimed: "It would be a mistake to suppose that the fate of Japan was settled by the atomic bomb. Her defeat was certain before the first atomic bomb fell and was brought about by overwhelming maritime power . . . There was no real need to use such a weapon (212)." He agreed with the U.S. Strategic Bombing Survey that Japan would in any case have surrendered before the year was out.

On the other hand, Stimson believed: "Our great objective was thus achieved, and all the evidence I have seen indicates that the controlling factor in the final Japanese decision to accept our terms of surrender was the atomic bomb (213)." A Japanese diplomat put a middle point of view: "It is certain that we would have surrendered in due time, even without the terrific chastisement of the bomb, or the terrible shock of the Russian attack. However, it cannot be denied that both the bombs and the Russians facilitated our surrender (214)."

Even if Japan had surrendered at the end of 1945, thousands more American soldiers would have been killed. Those responsible for dropping the bombs claimed not only that they had won the war, but that they saved many lives on both sides. According to Secretary of State Byrnes, "In those two raids there were many casualties, but not nearly so many as there would have been had our air force continued to drop incendiary bombs on Japan's cities. Certainly, by bringing the war to an end, the atomic bomb saved the lives of thousands of American boys (215)." *Counting the casualties*

The March fire raids on Tokyo had been devastating. Karl Compton wrote: "One of these raids killed about 125,000 people, the other nearly 100,000. Of the 210 square miles of greater Tokyo, 85 square miles of the densest part was destroyed as completely as were the centres of Hiroshima and Nagasaki (216)."

According to Stimson, the difference between the fire raids and the atomic raids was not the numbers or the cause of deaths. Rather it was the terrifying impact of so much damage by one single bomb, and the human fear of more such bombs to come: "The two atomic bombs which we had dropped were the only ones we had ready and our rate of production at the time was very small . . . But so far as the Japanese could know our ability to execute atomic attacks was unlimited . . . The atomic bomb was more than a weapon of terrible destruction. It was a psychological weapon (217)." Karl Compton agreed: "It was the experience of what an atomic bomb will actually do to a community plus the dread of many more, that was effective (218)."

To these men the atomic bomb was just one more military weapon. It was different in degree, but not in kind, from others used before. Henry Stimson wrote: "At no time, from 1941 to 1945, did I ever hear it suggested by the President or by any other responsible member of the government that atomic energy should not be used in the war ... We were at war, and the work must be done ... The possible atomic weapon was considered to be a new and tremendously powerful explosive, as legitimate as any other of the deadly explosive weapons of modern war. If victory could be speeded up by using the bomb, it should be used (219)." The idea of the bomb as just one more weapon was fairly generally held. Interviewed by the Mass Observation team, one young Englishman said, "We're absolutely right to use it. I've had some of that kind of thing in London myself." And another, "Well, it's only what we went through ourselves (220)."

Others argued that the new bomb was different in kind from anything used before. The Bishop of Chelmsford in the House of Lords did so on the ground that indiscriminate bombing of civilians was something both horrible and new. Admiral Leahy felt that, in using the bomb first, Americans "had adopted an ethical standard common to the barbarians of the Dark Ages. I was not taught to make war in that fashion, and wars cannot be won by destroying women and children (221)."

The public did not realize that the Allies were already bombing civilian as well as military targets. The terrible bombing of Hamburg and Dresden had been quite indiscriminate. Many even imagined that Hiroshima was itself a military target. In Britain one man told an interviewer: "They're all military zones, aren't they? This city was. They're all like Aldershot and Chatham. I don't say they would be right to use it on civilians (222)."

Truman fully agreed with Secretary Stimson's attitude: "Let there be no mistake about it. I regarded the bomb as a military weapon and never had any doubt that it should be used (223)." Churchill's feelings were the same: "To avert a vast butchery ... to give peace to the world, to lay healing hands upon its tortured peoples by a manifestation of overwhelming power at the cost of a few explosions, seemed, after all our toils and perils, a miracle of deliverance ... The historic fact remains ... that the decision whether or not to use the atomic bomb to compel the surrender of Japan was never even an issue (224)."

Churchill told the House of Commons on August 16th: "There are voices which assert that the bomb should never have been used at all. I cannot associate myself with such ideas . . . I am surprised that very worthy people, but people who in most cases had no intention of proceeding to the Japanese front themselves, should adopt the position that rather than throw this bomb, we should have sacrificed a million American and a quarter of a million British lives in the desperate battles and massacres of an invasion of Japan (225)."

Clement Attlee pointed out later, perhaps naively, "At the time we knew nothing . . . about the consequences of dropping the bomb, except that it was larger than an ordinary bomb and had a much greater explosive force . . . We knew nothing whatever at that time about the genetic effect of an atomic explosion. I knew nothing about fall-out and all the rest of what emerged after Hiroshima. As far as I know President Truman and Winston Churchill knew nothing of these things either, nor did Sir John Anderson . . . Whether the scientists directly concerned knew, or guessed, I do not know. But if they did, then, so far as I am aware, they said nothing of it to those who had to make the decision (226)." *Attlee*

The radiation effect of a possible bomb had been stressed in the Frisch-Peierls note of April, 1940: "It is difficult to tell what will happen to the radioactive material after the explosion. Most of it will probably be blown into the air and carried away by the wind. This cloud of radioactive material will kill everybody within a strip estimated to be several miles long . . . If one per cent of the active material sticks to the debris of, say, a square mile, any person entering this area would be in serious danger, even several days after the explosion (227)." It was only at Peierl's insistence that radiation had been even mentioned in the Maud Report. During the work on the Manhattan project the violence of the explosion had always been stressed far more than the prospect of radiation. Even the New Mexico test had not given the scientists much idea of what an atomic explosion would do to a living city. *Radiation problem*

So the moral issue was a far more prominent one after Hiroshima than before it. Twenty years later Group Captain Leonard Cheshire *Moral issue*

Emperor Hirohito, here inspecting incendiary-bomb damage in Tokyo, surrendered Japan after Hiroshima and Nagasaki

wrote: "To those who dropped the atom bomb the one reality was the war—the most terrible war the world has yet known. In their minds only two questions mattered: would the bomb end the war? Would it cost fewer lives than the one alternative, an all-out invasion of Japan? Undeniably, the answer to both questions was yes ... Today the emphasis has shifted. It is the dead of Hiroshima and Nagasaki, not the suffering that the world was spared, nor even the tyranny and evil with which it was threatened, who have become the one lasting reality and it is in their light the bomb is now judged (228)."

As reports from Hiroshima and Nagasaki filtered in, many people challenged the morality of the dropping of the bombs. The *New York Times* carried a report of an appeal to President Truman by thirty-four clergymen "that he order immediate discontinuance of production of atom bombs ... Condemning the atom bomb as 'an atrocity of a new magnitude' the statement asserted that by these acts Americans had 'descended step by step to an equally low level

100

of moral culpability' with the Japanese whom we had condemned for the bombing of Chinese cities (229)."

General Groves' secretary was shunned by her family when they found out what her secret war work had been. Enrico Fermi received a severe letter from his sister in Italy: "Everybody is talking about the atomic bomb, of course! People of good judgment abstain from a technical comment, and realize that it would be vain to seek who is the first author in a work which is the result of a vast collaboration. All, however, are perplexed and appalled by its dreadful effects, and with time the bewilderment increases rather than diminishes. For my part I recommend you to God who alone can judge you morally (230)." There is little evidence that Fermi, or the other scientists who had advised Stimson, regretted their decision. Those who were against using the bomb, like Leo Szilard and Franck, had pleaded in vain.

One of the Hiroshima pilots took a heavy personal burden of *The pilot's* guilt upon himself. Claude Eatherly had flown *Straight Flush*, the *despair* weather plane which had given the go ahead to Tibbets in the *Enola Gay*. On returning home, Eatherly rejected the hero's welcome given to the other pilots. He married, and took a job with an oil company. But he could not get the burned victims of Hiroshima out of his mind. He wrote streams of letters to the press and to survivors. He was haunted by nightmares, and in 1950 tried to commit suicide. After some time in a mental hospital he tried all ways of drawing attention to himself and to the great guilt he felt he was bearing on behalf of all Americans. He forged, and robbed, but no one would give him the satisfaction of pronouncing him guilty: he was told he was ill. He received a letter from Hiroshima: "We are all girls who escaped death fortunately, but received injuries in our faces, limbs and bodies from the atomic bomb . . . We heard recently that you have been tormented by a sense of guilt after the Hiroshima incident . . . This letter comes to you to convey our sincere sympathy with you and to assure you that we now do not harbour any sense of enmity to you personally (231)."

But Dr. Sasaki, trying to restore his hospital in Hiroshima, remarked: "I see that they are holding a trial for war criminals . . . I think they ought to try the men who decided to use the bomb and they should hang them all (232)."

8 Finger on the Trigger

THE MONTH FOLLOWING Hiroshima and Nagasaki, an influential American journal declared: "The world can never again be the same. A revolution has taken place under our bewildered gaze (233)." In Britain, Prime Minister Clement Attlee told the House of Commons: "We have been living through great events and we have got to realize we are living in a new world . . . We shall have to make a revaluation, especially in the sphere of international relations (234)."

The most worrying aspect of the postwar world was the rising tension between Russia and the Western Allies. Niels Bohr had seen in 1944 how atomic secrecy by America and Britain would heighten this tension (Chapter 5). Bohr's persuasions had failed, as had those of James Franck.

But others now took up his plea that only international atomic control could keep the world at peace. Attlee wrote to Truman the day "Fat Man" destroyed Nagasaki: "There is widespread anxiety as to whether the new power will be used to serve or destroy civilization . . . You and I, as heads of the governments which have control of this great force, should without delay make a joint declaration of our intentions to utilize the existence of this great power—not for our own ends but as trustees for humanity . . . in order to promote peace and justice in the world. The problems of control and the effect of the existence of this power on the new world organization will require careful consideration (235)."

The "new world organization" was the United Nations, set up at San Francisco in the spring of 1945. Each power on the U.N. Security Council had a right of veto. A British politician pointed out: "The Security Council cannot possibly exist if two permanent members of the Council possess so important a military secret that the other three have not got . . . It would only be a matter of time before some other scientist working for some other government manages to split some other atom and produces some other bomb. They will think that their bomb is better than ours, the temptation to test it will be irresistible, we shall have another war very quickly. I urge that the information should be handed over as soon as the United Nations charter has come into operation (236)." A colleague emphasized: "Unless and until that happens, we shall have to cherish this secret and hope for peace. But we shall be living in an uneasy world (237)."

The House of Commons was not unanimous about the matter. Winston Churchill told them: "So far as we know there are at least three years before the concrete progress made in the United States can be overtaken. In these three years we must remould the relationships of all men, wherever they dwell . . . I am in entire agreement with the President that the secrets of the atomic bomb shall so far as possible not be imparted at the present time to any other country in the world (238)."

For Truman had little sympathy with Attlee's letter, or with his own Secretary of War. To Henry Stimson, relations with Russia were "virtually dominated by the problem of the atomic bomb. Except for the problem of the control of that bomb, those relations might not be immediately pressing . . . But with the discovery of the bomb they become immediately emergent. Those relations may be perhaps irretrievably embittered by the way in which we approach the solution of the bomb with Russia. For if we fail to approach them now . . . having this weapon rather ostentatiously on our hip, their suspicions . . . of our purposes will increase. Whether Russia gets control of the necessary secret of production in a minimum of say, four years or a maximum of twenty years is not nearly as important to the world and civilization as to make sure that when they do get it they are willing and co-operative partners (239)."

The President, however, thought differently: "The destruction at Hiroshima and Nagasaki was lesson enough for me. The world could not afford to risk war with atomic weapons. But until a practical and foolproof method of control could be found it was

American atomic secrets

U.S.A. Atomic Energy Commission

103

important to retain the advantage which possession of the bomb had given us. In other words it was now more than ever necessary to guard and maintain the secrecy of the bomb (240)."

The United States Atomic Energy Commission was set up. It was to control all atomic work in America under strict security regulations. Clearly, Truman did not wish to share atomic secrets even with his closest Allies. This was against the spirit of the Quebec Agreement of 1943 (Chapter 3). The Hyde Park agreement of 1944 (Chapter 5) had also stated that: "Full collaboration between the United States and the British Government in developing Tube Alloys for military and commercial purposes should continue after the defeat of Japan, unless and until terminated by joint agreement (241)."

But since the Hyde Park conversations President Roosevelt had died. The record of the talks with Churchill had been lost. Admiral Leahy, who was present, later claimed: "There have been reports since that Roosevelt agreed to share the bomb's secret with Britain, but no such understanding was reached at this particular conference (242)." Attlee later told a journalist that the Quebec Agreement "was really rather a loose agreement. Practically Winston said to the Americans, 'You can have all the peaceful developments'. I think we could have claimed more. We had given a great deal through our experts. We contributed a great deal in fundamental research . . . No doubt it seemed a nice gesture not to bother about industrial use, or even to insist on too much specific exchange on the military side. We were Allies and friends. It didn't seem necessary to tie everything up (243)."

Attlee meets Truman   In 1945, newly elected British Prime Minister Attlee felt more aggrieved about America's failure to keep to the Quebec Agreement. The first Allied meeting of Foreign Ministers was taking place in London. Russian jealousy of the American monopoly of atomic power prevented its progress. As soon as it was over, Attlee flew with Sir John Anderson—chairman of the new U.K. Advisory Committee on Atomic Energy—to Washington to remonstrate with Truman. They met on the Presidential yacht, the *Williamsburg*. Anderson wrote to his wife: "At first we just sat around and gossiped in little groups while the boat went down stream . . . The President was most genial and showed me through two huge albums of photographs of his Potsdam trip. We then lunched on lobster salad, soup, turkey and soufflé surprise (244)."

The goodwill lasted. Three days later, the President and Prime Minister announced: "We agree that there should be full and effective co-operation in the field of atomic energy between the United States, the United Kingdom and Canada." More important, they advocated a United Nations Atomic Energy Commission: "We are not convinced that the spreading of the specialized information regarding the practical application of atomic energy, before it is possible to devise effective, reciprocal and enforceable safeguards acceptable to all nations, would contribute to a constructive solution of the problem of the atomic bomb . . . We are, however, prepared to share detailed information concerning the practical industrial application of atomic energy . . . A commission should be set up under the United Nations Organization to prepare recommendations for submission to the Organization (245)."

The first session of the General Assembly of the United Nations was held in London in January, 1946. The setting up of a U.N. Atomic Energy Commission was unanimously approved. But the Williamsburg agreement had not ended Russian suspicions. They vetoed the proposals for control. The deadlock strengthened those in the United States who had opposed the Anglo-American agreement. The Combined Policy Committee refused to tell Britain anything about the atomic energy plants in the States. Attlee wrote to Truman: "I am gravely disturbed at the turn which discussions have taken over the implementation of the document which you and I signed. As you know, the document stated that there should be full and effective co-operation in the field of atomic energy . . . and it seems to me that this cannot mean less than full interchange of information (246)." *Russia vetoes nuclear controls*

But Truman was now at odds with his Senate. Before the General Assembly meeting, a group of senators led by McMahon had introduced a Bill to place atomic energy under civilian control; the passing of information to foreign powers was to be banned. In August, 1946, the McMahon Act became law. Attlee said: "The Senate wanted to have everything for America. Once Congress proceeded to pass the McMahon Bill we had to go ahead on our own . . . We had to hold up our position *vis-à-vis* the Americans . . . *McMahon Act (U.S.A.)*

We had to bear in mind that there was always the possibility of their withdrawing and becoming isolationist once again. The manufacture of a British atom bomb was therefore at that stage essential to our defence . . . We had worked from the start for international control of the bomb. That was the best way. But it was obviously going to take a long time. Meanwhile we had to face the world as it was (247)."

Harwell and Windscale

Britain's Atomic Energy Act, passed in the autumn of 1946, empowered the Ministry of Supply to act. Anderson's Advisory Committee made the decisions. The research establishment already set up at Harwell in Berkshire was expanded. At Windscale in Cumberland two huge graphite-moderated reactors were built, together with a plant for extracting plutonium.

Acheson condemns atomic war

Meanwhile, following the abortive General Assembly meeting, Truman set up a special committee under Secretary of State Dean Acheson. It was to make a plan for atomic control. Acheson formed an advisory panel under David E. Lilienthal. The Acheson-Lilienthal report wanted all existing atomic bombs to be destroyed. The report was published on 28th March, 1946. Acheson broadcast to the American public: "In plain words the report sets up a plan under which no nation would make atomic bombs, or the materials for them. All dangerous activities would be carried on—not merely inspected—by a live functioning international authority with a real purpose in the world, and capable of attracting competent personnel. This monopoly of the dangerous activities would still leave a large and tremendously productive field of safe activities open to individual nations, their industries and universities... The extremely favoured position with regard to atomic devices which the United States enjoys at present is only temporary. It will not last. We must use that advantage now to promote international security, and to carry out our policy of building a lasting peace through international agreement (248)."

The U.S. senator presenting the report told United Nations members: "We are here to make a choice between the quick and the dead (249)." But the Russians relished neither the proposed measures of inspection, nor the sanctions—which included the loss of the right of veto. Molotov, for Russia, refused to vote. Next June the Western powers turned down Russia's proposal that all atomic projects should be inspected by a U.N. commission. A new mood of scepticism prevailed, caught by the American poet, Robert Frost (250):

> *Having invented a new holocaust,*
> *And been the first with it to win a war,*
> *How they make haste to cry with fingers crossed,*
> *Kings X—no fairs to use it any more.*

With the United Nations deadlock and the passing of the McMahon Act, international relations grew more strained. Russia refused to evacuate Manchuria, and accused Britain and France of keeping troops in the Middle East, Greece and Indonesia. The two

Iron curtain

Britain's Atomic Energy research establishment at Harwell, Berkshire

Above The explosion of a United States atomic bomb near the island of Bikini in the South Seas (1st July, 1946). *Below:* German labourers load sacks of flour onto a plane during the air lift to Berlin, blockaded by the Russians due to a dispute over its control (1948)

great *blocs*—East and West—were already carving out opposing spheres of influence. Just after the end of the European war Churchill asked Truman: "What is to happen about Russia? An iron curtain is drawn down upon their front (251)." A year later he told an audience in Missouri: "From Stettin in the Baltic to Trieste in the Adriatic, an iron curtain has descended across the continent ... All those famous cities and the populations around them lie in what I must call the Soviet sphere, and all are subject not only to Soviet influence but to a very high degree ... of control from Moscow (252)."

Tension rose. America exploded another test bomb in the South Seas near the island of Bikini. In June, 1947, she tried to extend her influence in Europe by offering economic aid under the Marshall plan. The Russian newspaper *Pravda* claimed that the plan "is only a repetition of the Truman plan for political pressure with the help of dollars, a plan for interference in the domestic affairs of other countries (253)." In September, Russia retaliated by setting up the Communist Information Bureau—the "Cominform"—to persuade the eastern European states into the Communist system. The February Communist *coup d'état* in Czechoslovakia increased western fears of Russian domination.

Marshall aid and Cominform

The Russians, for their part, feared that the Marshall plan would allow the West to integrate western Germany into western Europe; Berlin would become a capitalist outpost inside eastern Germany. The Allies had divided Germany into British, American, French and Russian zones. Berlin, in the middle of the Russian zone, had itself been split into four parts. Each part was governed by one of the Allies. In June, 1948, the Russians refused to join in this four power control of Berlin. They vetoed proposed currency reforms. Road and rail traffic were forbidden to enter the city from the west.

Berlin blockade

What were the Allies to do about the blockade? If they did nothing, Berlin would have to buy everything from the East; the city would fall completely under Russia's sway. An American general in Germany advised Truman, "If we withdraw, our position in Europe is threatened. If America does not understand this now, does not know that the issue is cast, then it never will and Communism will run rampant (254)." He wanted to use troops to force open the land routes into Berlin. Luckily the Allies did not take his advice. Instead, they mounted a gigantic air lift. Planes brought food and necessities into West Berlin at the rate of more than one aircraft per minute for eight months.

N.A.T.O   The western Allies formed a defensive pact, the North Atlantic Treaty Organization. N.A.T.O. and Cominform countries were drawn up on either side of the "iron curtain" as Churchill had called it. The gap between their respective strengths was closed just as Russia lifted the Berlin blockade. On September 23rd Truman announced: "I believe the American people, to the fullest extent consistent with national security, are entitled to be informed of all developments in the field of atomic energy. That is my reason for making public the following information. We have evidence that within recent weeks an atomic explosion occurred within the U.S.S.R. Ever since atomic energy was first released by man the eventual development of this new force by other nations has been expected (255)."

Russia's first   The same announcement was issued from 10 Downing Street, and
test bomb   reported in the British press. The *Daily Mirror* ran banner headlines. "Atomic Blast in Russia: Russia now knows how to make an atomic bomb." The *Mirror*'s Washington correspondent cabled that "While the British people took the A-bomb news calmly there was great excitement in America. Radio network announcers broke into musical programmes. Newsboys shouting—'The Russians have the bomb'—quickly sold out to people queuing for special editions of the newspaper. Most scientists and statesmen were not surprised by the news (256)."

Nuclear   Admiral Leahy commented: "Perhaps there is some hope that
deterrent   its capacity for death and terror among the defenceless may restrain nations from using the atom bomb against each other (257)." Otto Hahn, the scientist who had first split the atom ten years before, told a journalist: "I am glad. If both sides have the bomb there will be no war. It will be just as with gas in the last war. Neither side used it as they knew the others had it too (258)." Neither the Americans nor the Russians used their atomic bombs during the Korean war which began six months later.

Before the Korean War was over the British in 1952 exploded their own atomic bomb. That November the first hydrogen bomb—on which Edward Teller had begun work at Los Alamos—was
110   exploded in the Eniwetok area of the Pacific. Within a year Russia

announced the successful test of her first hydrogen bomb. In 1957 Britain followed suit; in 1960 France produced an atomic bomb. Nuclear arms were proliferating. As the arms race speeded up, the public debate grew fiercer. The defenders of the nuclear weapons, with the huge budgets they entailed, argued that they would deter any power thinking of war. Others believed that if the weapons were made they would certainly be used.

They also feared the effects of the atomic fall-out produced by the testing of so many bombs by so many nations. Strontium 90, a radioactive fission product, could be carried into the upper air from a nuclear blast and fall on the earth thousands of miles away. It would contaminate soil, plants, animals and their produce, and become concentrated in human bones. Many people feared this fall-out. A fictional character exclaimed: "What about these tests! Isn't it enough to you that every three seconds somewhere a baby

Strontium 90

Labour Party Member of Parliament Michael Foot (*centre*) heading a march of the Campaign for Nuclear Disarmament to London from the atomic weapons research establishment at Aldermaston, Berkshire

dies of starvation? Have we got to spend millions every year to kill the rest? Let's have less about freedom and more about strontium 90 in my kids' bones. Thousands of people are going to die of this new bomb even if it doesn't go off (259)."

Reports reached the West of a high rate of thyroid cancer among those who had been near Hiroshima and Nagasaki. There were stories, too, of malformed children born to survivors. A scientist wrote: "In my opinion we cannot today make any useful quantitative assessment of the genetic consequences of exposure of human populations to ionizing radiations at low dosage rates. We know far too little about human population structure and the induction of mutations in man. But we know enough to be apprehensive about the genetic dangers! (260)"

Aldermaston marches   In Britain, these fears were voiced by the Campaign for Nuclear Disarmament. Initiated by a few well-known personalities of the left including Canon Collins, the novelist J. B. Priestley, the historian A. J. P. Taylor and the left-wing Labour M. P. Michael Foot C.N.D. demanded the end of the making and testing of nuclear weapons. It was ignored by the government and frowned upon by the so-called "establishment". But the first C.N.D. Easter march to the atomic weapons research establishment at Aldermaston, Berkshire, attracted wide support and publicity. The press carried pictures of the columns of marchers of all ages and descriptions, carrying banners, children, and their food for three days. At a Trafalgar Square rally in London they "heard Michael Foot vow that the campaign would be carried on all over the country, forcing demands upon the politicians 'until these fearful machines at Aldermaston are dismantled, until we get a British government that gives a real lead to the nations.' (261)"

Nuclear escalation   But C.N.D. failed. The arms race continued. "Escalation" became a fashionable word; each side rushed to build bigger and better weapons than the other. By 1967 the United States had 1,054 land-based missiles able to deliver nuclear warheads, 656 submarines equipped with Poseidon warheads twice as powerful as "Little Boy", and a whole fleet of B.52 bombers designed to carry hydrogen bombs. In the 1970s sporadic attempts at international control have been less successful than the continued nuclear stockpiling. Each American "minuteman" warhead in its silo, sixty feet below the

H.M.S. *Renown*, the Royal Navy's third Polaris submarine at Port Canaverel, Cape Kennedy, for test missile firings (17 July, 1969)

ground, can on the orders of the President be released to kill 80 million people. The Russians have enormous missiles capable of attacking the "minutemen"; and the Americans are making weapons with multiple warheads to overcome the anti-ballistic missiles ranged around Moscow.

Early on, scientists saw the huge potential of atomic energy for good as well as for destruction. After the bombing of Hiroshima a leader writer commented: "It is the pressure of war itself that has forced ahead a process which can be turned against war in the long run and at the same time promises a greater material enrichment of

Atoms for peace

A United States "minuteman" missile is successfully fired on a test launch
from its underground silo in California (9th May, 1960)

life than any single scientific discovery before it (262)." Radioactive
isotopes have been used since the war in farming and medicine.
Plans for harnessing atomic energy to generate power for industry
are going ahead.

Doomsday   Meanwhile, as the arms race continues, the threat of the mushroom cloud seems ironically to have receded to the back of the
public's mind. Science fiction, with films like *Dr. Strangelove* and
novels like *Fail Safe*, has converted the nightmare into grim—even
sick—entertainment. They act as safety valves. Many claim that the
bombing of Hiroshima not only saved lives in 1945 but acted as a
deterrent to another full-scale war. They hope it will continue to
do so.

Others are less hopeful: "Sooner or later one country's going to
use it against another. Maybe in 20 years, maybe in 100. Maybe not
for 200 or 1,000 years. But sooner or later it'll be too much of a
temptation . . . You can just blow a corner off the world. Eventually
it'll be just like one of those fantastic tales . . . Just a few people left
in caves. It'll reduce the whole of so-called civilization to living in
114   caves (263)."

Further Reading

THE OFFICIAL HISTORIES of the British and American atomic projects are Margaret Gowing's *Britain and Atomic Energy: 1939–45*, (Macmillan, London, 1964; St. Martin Press, New York, 1964), and *The New World 1939–46* (Pennsylvania State University Press, 1962) by R. G. Hewlett and O. E. Anderson. Another excellent political commentary on the production and use of the bomb is Volume VI in J. Ehrman's and J. R. M. Butler's *Grand Strategy* (H.M.S.O., London, 1957). A journalistic approach makes Michael Amrine's *The Great Decisions* (Heinemann, London, 1960; Putnam, New York, 1955) and William L. Laurence's *Dawn over Zero* (Museum Press, London, 1948; Alfred Knopf, New York, 1946) less objective but equally readable. *Japan Subdued* (Oxford University Press, 1961; Princeton University Press, 1961) by Herbert Feis describes in detail both Japanese and American motives in the last stages of the war.

The different accounts of those involved in policy making include William D. Leahy's *I Was There* (Gollancz, London, 1950; McGraw-Hill, New York, 1950), James Byrnes' *Speaking Frankly* (Heinemann, London, 1947; Harper & Row, New York, 1947) and Harry Truman's *Year of Decision*, Volume I of the "Memoirs" (Hodder & Stoughton, London, 1955; Doubleday, New York, 1955). Winston Churchill's attitude to the bomb comes out very clearly in the last volume of his *History of the Second World War, Triumph and Tragedy* (Cassell, London, 1954; Houghton Mifflin, New York, 1954). Sir John Wheeler Bennett's *John Anderson, Viscount Waverley* (Macmillan, London, 1962) is interesting on Anglo-American relations. Another useful biography is Ruth Moore's *Niels Bohr* (Hodder & Stoughton, London, 1967; Alfred Knopf, New York, 1966). The official scientific account of the project, *Atomic Energy for Military Purposes* (Oxford University Press, London, 1946; Princeton University Press, New York, 1946) by Henry de Wolf Smyth is beautifully clear and readable. Also helpful are James Baxter's *Scientists against Time* (M.I.T. Press, London, 1968) and Arthur Compton's *Atomic Quest* (Oxford University Press, New York and London, 1956).

General L. R. Groves' *Now It Can be Told* (Andre Deutsch, London, 1963; Harper & Row, New York, 1961) is self revealing as well as a fascinating account of the actual organization of the atomic project. *We Dropped the Atom Bomb* (Thomas Crowell, New York, 1946) by Merle Miller and Ave Spitzer describes some of the pilots' experiences. The fate of the victims is best recorded by John Hersey whose article for the *New Yorker* was reprinted as *Hiroshima* (Penguin, London, 1946; Alfred Knopf, New York, 1946). Robert Jungk's *Children of the Ashes* (Heinemann, London, 1961; Harcourt Brace, New York, 1961) describes the lives of some of the survivors. *Brighter than a Thousand Suns* (Gollancz, London 1958; Harcourt Brace, New York, 1958) by the same author is a biased but intensely readable account of the whole period.

Few contemporary novelists have taken the bomb as a direct theme. C. P. Snow's *The New Men* (Macmillan, London, 1954; Scribner, New York, 1955) catches the excitement of the scientific discoveries and the agony of the scientists' moral dilemma. *Fail Safe* (Hutchinson, London, 1963; McGraw-Hill, New York, 1962) by Eugene Burdick and Harvey Wheeler is a graphic warning of what could happen.

Table of Events

1938

December 22nd   Otto Hahn publishes paper on uranium bombardment; the atom split.

1939

March 15th   German troops occupy Prague, Czechoslovakia
March 16th   Enrico Fermi warns U.S. Navy Department of German nuclear research
August 2nd   Einstein signs letter to President Roosevelt calling for nuclear bomb research
September 1st   Germany invades Poland
                Bohr-Wheeler papers on uranium isotopes published
September 3rd   Britain declares war on Hitler's Germany

1940

April   Peierls-Frisch memorandum on the nuclear chain reaction bomb
                Maud Committee set up in Britain to research the atomic bomb

1941

June 28th   Roosevelt establishes Office of Scientific Research and Development under Dr. Vannevar Bush
July 11th   Discovery of plutonium reported
July 15th   Maud Report says the bomb is possible
October 17th   Tube Alloys set up by British Government to develop the bomb

December 6th	Roosevelt announces all-out-effort to produce atomic bomb
December 7th	Japanese attack Pearl Harbor and bring America into the war

1942

June 21st	Hyde Park talks between Churchill and Roosevelt for the pooling of scientific resources
August 13th	"Manhattan District" (U.S. army atomic development unit) formed
September 17th	General Groves given command of Manhattan project
December 2nd	Fermi achieves nuclear chain reaction in Chicago

1943

January 14th	Churchill complains to Roosevelt at Casablanca that America is excluding Britain from atomic research projects
February 28th	Norwegian heavy water plant destroyed; Nazi nuclear effort sabotaged
April 6th	Construction of Hanford plutonium piles begins in America
August 19th	Quebec Agreement for Anglo-American atomic secrets sharing

1944

May 16th	Niels Bohr warns Churchill of dangers of atomic warfare to mankind
July 3rd	Bohr warns Roosevelt of dangers of atomic warfare

September 19th Hyde Park Agreement between Churchill and Roosevelt that the bomb should be kept secret from the outside world

1945

April 12th	Roosevelt dies and Truman becomes U.S. President
May 9th	U.S. Interim Committee meets under Secretary of War Henry Stimson to discuss bombing of Japan
May 9th	President Truman announces Germany's surrender
May 16th	Pilots arrive at Tinian Island to prepare for Hiroshima
June 11th	Franck Report
July 15th	Victorious Allies begin the Potsdam Conference
July 16th	American test bomb exploded in New Mexico
July 26th	America delivers ultimatum to Japan
August 6th	Uranium bomb dropped on Hiroshima
August 8th	Russia declares war on Japan
	Plutonium bomb dropped on Nagasaki
August 14th	Japan surrenders
November 15th	Williamsburg Declaration: America and Britain declare co-operation and call for a United Nations Atomic Energy Commission

1946

January 24th	First session of United Nations General Assembly
March 28th	Acheson-Lilienthal Report
July 1st	Bikini test bomb exploded
August 1st	McMahon Act makes American atomic research secret

1947

June 5th   Marshall Aid Plan for Postwar Europe announced
                  by the U.S.A.
September   Cominform set up by Russia to strengthen the
                  Eastern bloc

1948

May 17th   Atomic Energy Commission of U.N. recommends
                  its own suspension
June 18th   Russia begins blockade of Berlin

1949

April 4th   North Atlantic Treaty Organization formed
September 23rd   First Russian atomic bomb announced

1950

June 25th   Invasion of South Korea by North Koreans

1952

November 1st   U.S. hydrogen bomb exploded

1953

August 12th   Russians announce explosion of hydrogen bomb

Notes on Sources

(1) William Laurence, *Dawn over Zero* (1947)

(2) White Paper on Statements relating to the Atom Bomb, 12th August, 1945

(3) Arthur Compton, *Atomic Quest* (1956)

(4) White Paper on Statements relating to the Atom Bomb, 12th August, 1945

(5) Royal Institute Speech, 6th June, 1919

(6) Ernest Rutherford to Niels Bohr, 9th December, 1917

(7) *Nature*, 6th November, 1919

(8) Niels Bohr lecture, Stockholm, 11th December, 1922

(9) *Nature*, 27th February, 1932

(10) *Sunday Express*, 30th April, 1939

(11) *Nature*, 16th June, 1934

(12) Laura Fermi, *Atoms in the Family* (1955)

(13) *Nature*, 19th May, 1934. Letter from Enrico Fermi dated 10th April, 1934

(14) *Times*, 5th June, 1934

(15) Laura Fermi, *Atoms in the Family* (1955)

(16) Paul Langevin, 1933. Quoted Robert Jungk, *Brighter than a Thousand Suns* (1956)

(17) *Sunday Express*, 30th April, 1939

(18) White Paper on Statements relating to the Atom Bomb, 12th August, 1945

(19) *Saturday Evening Post*, 7th September, 1940. William Laurence, "The Atom Gives Up"

(20) *Nature*, 11th February, 1939

(21) *Science Survey*, 28th January, 1939

(22) Harold Nicolson, *Public Faces* (1932)

(23) Enrico Fermi lecture, American Institute of Electrical Engineers, 24th January, 1940

(24) Leo Szilard to Frederic Joliot, 2nd February, 1939

(25) William Laurence, *Dawn over Zero* (1947)

(26) *New York Times*, 5th May, 1940

(27) Professor George Pegram to Admiral S. C. Hooper, Office of Chief Naval Operations, 16th March, 1939

(28) Albert Einstein to President Roosevelt, 2nd August, 1939

(29) *Saturday Evening Post*, 7th September, 1940. William Laurence, "The Atom Gives Up"

(30) *Sunday Express*, 30th April, 1939

(31) *Discovery*, September, 1939. C. P. Snow's editorial

(32) Winston Churchill to Kingsley Wood, 5th August, 1939. Quoted *The Gathering Storm* (1948)

(33) Frisch-Peierls Memorandum, April, 1940

(34) White Paper on Statements relating to the Atom Bomb, 12th August, 1945

(35) C. P. Snow, *The New Men* (1954)

(36) White Paper on Statements relating to the Atom Bomb, 12th August, 1945

(37) Maud Report, July, 1940

(38) Lord Cherwell minute to Winston Churchill, 27th August, 1941

(39) Winston Churchill to Lord Ismay, 31st August, 1941

(40) Report of Defence Service Panel of Scientific Advisory Committee, 25th September, 1941

(41) Francis Williams, *A Prime Minister Remembers* (1961)

(42) President Roosevelt to Winston Churchill, 11th October, 1941

(43) Order establishing O.S.R.D., 28th June, 1941

(44) *Saturday Evening Post*, 7th September, 1940. William Laurence, "The Atom Gives Up"

(45) Ernest Lawrence memorandum to Committee of National Academy of Sciences, 11th July, 1941

(46) Arthur Compton, *Atomic Quest* (1956)

(47) Report of Committee of National Academy of Sciences, 6th November, 1941

(48) Arthur Compton, *Atomic Quest* (1956)

(49) Margaret Gowing, *Britain and Atomic Energy 1939–45* (1964)

(50) *New York Times*, 8th December, 1941

(51) Bush's note of O.S. R.D. meeting 16th December 1941. Quoted James Baxter, *Scientists against Time* (1946)

(52) Report from W. Akers, quoted by Margaret Gowing, *Britain and Atomic Energy 1939–45* (1964)

(53) Pollard and Davidson, *Applied Nuclear Physics* (1942)

(54) James B. Conant memorandum to Vannevar Bush, 14th May, 1942

(55) White Paper on Statements relating to the Atom Bomb, 12th August, 1945

(56) Winston Churchill, *History of the Second World War*, Vol. 11, *The Hinge of Fate* (1951)

(57) Lord Ismay, *Memoirs* (1960)

(58) John Anderson memorandum to Winston Churchill, 30th July, 1942

(59) Leslie R. Groves, *Now It Can be Told* (1963)

(60) R. G. Hewlett & O. E. Anderson, *The New World 1939–46* (1962)

(61) Leslie R. Groves, *Now It Can be Told* (1963)

(62) Arthur Compton, *Atomic Quest* (1956)

(63) Henry de Wolfe Smyth, *Atomic Energy for Military Purposes* (1946)

(64) Leslie R. Groves, *Now It Can be Told* (1963)

(65) Winston Churchill cable to Harry Hopkins, 27th February, 1943

(66) Vannevar Bush memorandum to Harry Hopkins, 31st March, 1943

(67) Quebec Agreement, 19th August, 1943

(68) White Paper on Statements relating to the Atom Bomb, 12th August, 1945

(69) J. R. Oppenheimer to General Nichols, 4th May, 1954. Transcript of hearings before Personnel Security Board of U.S.A.E.C., April–May, 1954

(70) Leslie R. Groves to Manhattan District Engineer, 20th July, 1943

(71) Leslie R. Groves, *Now It Can be Told* (1963)

(72) J. R. Oppenheimer to General Nichols, 4th May, 1954. Transcript of hearings before Personnel Security Board of U.S.A.E.C., April–May, 1954

(73) Laura Fermi, *All About Atomic Energy* (1962)

(74) James Chadwick to Niels Bohr, quoted by Margaret Gowing, *Britain and Atomic Energy 1939–45* (1964)

(75) Niels Bohr to James Chadwick. *Ibid.*

(76) Laura Fermi, *All About Atomic Energy* (1962)

(77) Leslie R. Groves, *Now It Can be Told* (1963)

(78) Laura Fermi, *All About Atomic Energy* (1962)

(79) Harry S. Truman, *Year of Decision* (1955)

(80) William D. Leahy, *I Was There* (1950)

(81) J. R. Oppenheimer to General Nichols, 4th May, 1954. Transcript of hearings before Personnel Security Board of U.S.A.E.C., April–May, 1954

(82) Josef Goebbels, *Diary*, trans. & ed. Louis P. Lochner (1948). Entry 21st March, 1942

(83) Gunnerside Report. Entry 28th February, 1943. Quoted William Laurence, *Dawn over Zero* (1947)

(84) *Times*, 8th August, 1945

(85) Sir Alan Brooke to Major Nigel Aitken, 26th August, 1945

(86) Order establishing Alsos. Quoted Leslie R. Groves, *Now It Can be Told* (1963)

(87) Leslie R. Groves, *Now It Can be Told* (1963)

(88) Henry de Wolfe Smyth, *Atomic Energy for Military Purposes* (1946)

(89) Leslie R. Groves, *Now It Can be Told* (1963)

(90) U.S. Atomic Energy Commission report, L.A.M.S./2532, Vol. 1

(91) Leslie R. Groves, *Now It Can be Told* (1963)

(92) *Ibid.*

(93) William D. Leahy, *I Was There* (1950). Account of meeting 27th September, 1944

(94) Leslie R. Groves memorandum to General Marshall, 30th December, 1944

(95) *Ibid.*

(96) Leslie R. Groves, *Now It Can be Told* (1963)

(97) *Spectator*, 6th August, 1965. Group Captain Leonard Cheshire, "The Bomb in the Yellow Box"

(98) William Laurence, *Dawn over Zero* (1947)

(99) *Spectator*, 6th August, 1965. Group Captain Leonard Cheshire, "The Bomb in the Yellow Box"

(100) Dr. Philip Morrison's report to Senate Committee. Quoted William Laurence, *Dawn over Zero* (1947)

(101) *Harpers Magazine*, February, 1947. Henry L. Stimson, "Decision to use the Atom Bomb"

(102) Henry de Wolfe Smyth, *Atomic Energy for Military Purposes* (1946)

(103) Laura Fermi, *Atoms in the Family* (1955)

(104) William Laurence, *Dawn over Zero* (1947)

(105) General Farrell memorandum to Henry L. Stimson, 18th July, 1945

(106) Leslie R. Groves memorandum to Henry L. Stimson, 18th July, 1945

(107) *Spectator*, 6th August, 1965. Group Captain Leonard Cheshire, "The Bomb in the Yellow Box"

(108) *Ibid.*

(109) Leo Szilard to Robert Jungk. Quoted Robert Jungk, *Brighter than a Thousand Suns* (1956)

(110) John Anderson's memorandum to Winston Churchill, March, 1944

(111) Niels Bohr's memorandum to President Roosevelt, 3rd July, 1944

(112) Aide-memoire of Hyde Park Conversation, 19th September, 1944

(113) Henry L. Stimson to President Truman, 24th April, 1945

(114) Harry S. Truman, *Year of Decisions* (1955). Entry 25th April, 1945

(115) *New York Times*, 4th May, 1944

(116) Interim Committe Meeting minutes, 31st May, 1944

(117) Arthur Compton, *Atomic Quest* (1956)

(118) James Byrnes, *Speaking Frankly* (1947)

(119) Report of the Scientific Advisory Panel of Interim Committee, 9th June, 1945

(120) Arthur Compton, *Atomic Quest* (1956)

(121) Franck Report, 11th July, 1945

(122) Interim Committee Report, 16th June, 1945

(123) J. R. Oppenheimer to General Nichols, 4th May, 1954. Transcript of hearings before Personnel Security Board of U.S.A.E.C., April–May, 1954

(124) Poll of scientists, 12th July, 1945. Quoted Knebel & Bailey, *No High Ground* (1960)

(125) Field-Marshal Wilson to Sir John Anderson, 30th April, 1945

(126) Minutes of Combined Policy Committee meeting, 4th July, 1945

(127) Leslie R. Groves address to Los Alamos scientists, 24th December, 1944

(128) J. R. Oppenheimer to General Nichols, 4th May, 1954. Transcript of hearings before Personnel Security Board of U.S.A.E.C., April–May, 1954

(129) William D. Leahy, *I*

Was There (1950)

(130) *Harpers Magazine*, February, 1947. Henry L. Stimson, "Decision to use the Atom Bomb"

(131) Combined Intelligence Committee Report, July, 1945

(132) Harry S. Truman, *Year of Decisions* (1955)

(133) Henry L. Stimson's memorandum to President Truman, 2nd July, 1945

(134) *Atlantic Monthly*, October, 1960. Samuel E. Morison, "Why Japan Surrendered"

(135) Report of 18th June meeting of Peace Party, quoted by Toshikasu Kase, *Eclipse of the Rising Sun* (1951)

(136) Henry L. Stimson's memorandum to President Truman, 2nd July, 1945

(137) George Harrison cables to President Truman, 17th/18th July, 1945

(138) Winston Churchill, *History of the Second World War*, Vol. VI, *Triumph and Tragedy* (1953)

(139) *Atlantic Monthly*, March, 1957. Article by Harvey H. Bundy

(140) Winston Churchill, *History of the Second World War*, Vol. VI, *Triumph and Tragedy*

(141) Sir Alan Brooke's diary. Entry of 23rd

July, 1945. Arthur Bryant, *The Turn of the Tide* (1957)

(142) James Byrnes, *Speaking Frankly* (1947)

(143) Winston Churchill's note to Cabinet, 18th July, 1945

(144) Harry S. Truman, *Year of Decisions* (1955)

(145) Winston Churchill, *History of the Second World War*, Vol. VI, *Triumph and Tragedy*

(146) Harry S. Truman, *Year of Decisions* (1955)

(147) James Byrnes, *Speaking Frankly* (1947)

(148) Potsdam Declaration, 26th July, 1945

(149) William D. Leahy, *I Was There* (1950)

(150) James Byrnes, *Speaking Frankly* (1947)

(151) George Harrison cables to President Truman, 21st/23rd July, 1945

(152) President Truman to Professor Cate, 12th January, 1953. Professor Cate, *United States Army Air Forces in World War Two* (1948)

(153) Thomas Handy, General G.S.C. Acting Chief of Staff to General Carl Spaatz, C.G. U.S. Army Strategic Forces, 25th July, 1945

(154) Harry S. Truman, *Year of Decisions* (1955)

(155) Specifications to pilots, 4th August, 1945

(156) Colonel Tibbets' add-

ress to pilots, 5th August, 1945

(157) Harry Barnard, *Atomic Might — Ballad in honour of the 509th*

(158) Captain Lewis's log of *Enola Gay* flight, 6th August, 1945. Quoted by William Laurence, *Dawn over Zero* (1947)

(159) William S. Parsons' report to General Farrell, 6th August, 1945

(160) Citation for Colonel Tibbets' Distinguished Service Cross

(161) General Farrell to General Leslie R. Groves, 6th August, 1945

(162) *New Yorker*, August, 1946. John Hersey, "Hiroshima"

(163) Michihiko Hachiya, *Journal of a Japanese Physician*. Entry for 6th August, 1945

(164) *New Yorker*, August, 1946. John Hersey, "Hiroshima"

(165) Michihiko Hachiya, *Journal of a Japanese Physician*. Entry for 14th August, 1945

(166) *New Yorker*, August, 1946. John Hersey, "Hiroshima"

(167) *Ibid.*

(168) Michihiko Hachiya, *Journal of a Japanese Physician*. Entry for 7th August, 1945

(169) *Ibid.* Entry for 13th August, 1945

(170) *Ibid.*

(171) *New York Times*, 20th

124

August, 1945

(172) *New Yorker*, August, 1946. John Hersey, "Hiroshima"

(173) Michihiko Hachiya, *Journal of a Japanese Physician*. Entry for 11th August, 1945

(174) *New Yorker*, August, 1946. John Hersey, "Hiroshima"

(175) *Ibid.*

(176) *Ibid.*

(177) *Ibid.*

(178) *Ibid.*

(179) Michihiko Hachiya, *Journal of a Japanese Physician*. Entry for 21st August, 1945

(180) *Ibid.* Entry for 19th August, 1945

(181) *Ibid.* Entry for 22nd August, 1945

(182) *Ibid.* Entry for 8th September, 1945

(183) *Ibid.*

(184) William Laurence, *Dawn over Zero* (1947)

(185) U.S. Strategic Bombing Survey, 1946

(186) General Carl Spaatz's cable to President Truman, 6th August, 1945

(187) William D. Leahy, *I Was There* (1950)

(188) Presidential statement, 6th August, 1945

(189) Prime Minister's statement, 6th August, 1945

(190) Mass Observation, *Peace and the Public* (1947)

(191) John Lehmann, *I am My Brother* (1960)

(192) *New Statesman*, "London Diary", 11th August, 1945

(193) *Times*, 8th August, 1945

(194) Hermann Hagedorn, *The Bomb that fell on America* (1946)

(195) Dr. Bagge, Diary entry for 7th August, 1945. Quoted by Robert Jungk, *Brighter than a Thousand Suns* (1956)

(196) Japanese broadcast 6 a.m., 7th August, 1945

(197) *Daily Mirror*, 8th August, 1945

(198) Leaflet addressed to Japanese, 7th August, 1945

(199) William Laurence, *Dawn over Zero* (1947)

(200) Top Secret Field Order No. 17, 8th August, 1945

(201) Leslie R. Groves, *Now It Can be Told* (1963)

(202) William Laurence, *Dawn over Zero* (1947)

(203) Matsu Mariuchi, *We of Nagasaki* (1951). Account of Makoto Nagai

(204) *Ibid.* Account of Takasi Nagai

(205) *New York Times*, 11th August, 1945

(206) War Council minutes quoted by Toshikasu Kase, *Eclipse of the Rising Sun* (1951)

(207) *Ibid.*

(208) Sir Alan Brooke's *Diary*. Entry for 10th August, 1945. Arthur Bryant, *The Turn of the Tide* (1957)

(209) *Atlantic Monthly*, December, 1946. Karl Compton, "If the Atom Bomb had not been Used"

(210) Michihiku Hachiya, *Journal of a Japanese Physician*. Entry for 15th August, 1945

(211) Harry S. Truman, *Year of Decisions* (1955)

(212) Captain Sir Basil Liddell Hart, *History of the Second World War* (1970)

(213) *Harpers Magazine*, February, 1947. Henry L. Stimson, "Decision to use the Atom Bomb"

(214) Toshikasu Kase, *Journey to the Missouri* (1950)

(215) James Byrnes, *Speaking Frankly* (1947)

(216) *Atlantic Monthly*, December, 1946. Karl Compton, "If the Atomic Bomb had not been Used"

(217) *Harpers Magazine*, February, 1947. Henry L. Stimson, "Decision to use the Atom Bomb"

(218) *Atlantic Monthly*, December, 1946. Karl Compton, "If the Atomic Bomb had not been Used"

(219) *Harpers Magazine*, February, 1947. Henry L. Stimson, "Decision to use the Atom Bomb"

(220) Mass Observation, *Peace and the Public* (1947)

(221) William D. Leahy, *I Was There* (1950)
(222) Mass Observation, *Peace and the Public* (1947)
(223) Harry S. Truman, *Year of Decision* (1955)
(224) Winston Churchill, *History of the Second World War*, Vol. VI, *Triumph and Tragedy*
(225) Hansard, 16th August, 1945
(226) Francis Williams, *A Prime Minister Remembers* (1961)
(227) Frisch-Peierls Memorandum, April, 1940
(228) *Spectator*, 6th August, 1965. Group Captain Leonard Cheshire, "The Bomb in the Yellow Box"
(229) *New York Times*, 20th August, 1945
(230) Maria Fermi to Enrico Fermi, August, 1945. Quoted Laura Fermi, *Atoms in the Family* (1955)
(231) Girls of Hiroshima to Claude Eatherly, 24th July, 1959. Quoted Gunther Anders *Burning Conscience* (1961)
(232) *New Yorker*, August, 1946. John Hersey, "Hiroshima"
(233) *Saturday Review of Literature*, 15th September, 1945. Alma Johnson, "Education in an Atomic Age"
(234) *Hansard*, 16th August, 1945

(235) Clement Attlee to Harry S. Truman, 8th August, 1945
(236) *Hansard*, 20th August, 1945. Vernon Bartlett
(237) *Hansard*, 23rd August, 1945. Robert Boothby
(238) *Hansard*, 16th August, 1945
(239) Henry L. Stimson's memorandum to President Truman, 11th September, 1945
(240) Harry S. Truman, *Year of Decisions* (1955)
(241) Aide-memoire of Hyde Park conversation, 19th September, 1944
(242) William D. Leahy, *I Was There* (1950)
(243) Francis Williams, *A Prime Minister Remembers* (1961)
(244) John Anderson to Ava Anderson, 11th November, 1945
(245) Williamsburg Agreement, 15th November, 1945
(246) Clement Attlee to Harry S. Truman, 16th April, 1946
(247) Francis Williams, *A Prime Minister Remembers* (1961)
(248) Dean Acheson's broadcast of 28th March, 1946
(249) Bernard Baruch's address to U.N.A.E.C., 14th July, 1946
(250) *Atlantic Monthly*, December, 1946. Robert Frost, "Kings X"
(251) Winston Churchill's

telegram to Harry S. Truman, 12th May, 1945
(252) Winston Churchill at Fulton, Missouri, 5th March, 1946
(253) *Pravda*, 16th June, 1947. Quoted *Times*, 17th June, 1947
(254) General Clay on teletype record of conference, 16th April, 1949. Quoted E. du B. Clay, *Decision in Germany* (1950)
(255) Harry S. Truman speech, 23rd September, 1949
(256) *Daily Mirror*, 24th September, 1949
(257) William D. Leahy, *I Was There* (1950)
(258) *Daily Mirror*, 24th September, 1949
(259) Jennifer Dawson, *The Cold Country* (1965)
(260) *Bulletin of the Atomic Scientists*, December, 1955. T. C. Carter, "The Genetic Problem of Irradiated Human Populations"
(261) *Times*, 5th April, 1958
(262) *Times*, 8th August, 1945
(263) Mass Observation, *Peace and the Public* (1947)

Index

Picture Credits

128

The Publishers wish to thank the following for their kind permission to reproduce copyright illustrations on the pages mentioned: Trustees of the Imperial War Museum, *frontispiece*, 77, 85, 91, 92, 93, 95; Keystone Press Agency Ltd., 10 *bottom*, 32, 36, 37, 41, 52, 55, 67, 74, 75, 84, 86, 100, 108 *top*, 111, 114; Fox Photos Ltd., 10 *top*, 23, 113; the Radio Times Hulton Picture Library, 18, 107, 108 *bottom*; the Mansell Collection 80; the Hiroshima Peace Memorial Museum, 78, 82.